Humor is an
Attitude

SOMETIMES YOU JUST HAVE TO
LAUGH YOUR WAY OUT

JIM BOB SOLSBERY

Humor Is An Attitude
Sometimes You Just Have to Laugh Your Way Out

Jim Bob Solsbery

Published by:
Jim Bob Solsbery
16706 Blue Shine Trail
Cypress, TX 77433

jimbobspeaker@gmail.com
www.LaughYourWayOut.com

Cover design and interior layout: www.TheBookProducer.com
Printed in the United States of America

ISBN 978-0-9823748-0-1

To my wife, Jan, for her love and friendship...and for her encouragement...and for her laughing with me... and for her ability to help me through my "computer challenged" moments without saying, "You moron – any second grader I teach could do this!"

CONTENTS

PROLOGUE

"The woods are full of people that learned to write but evidently can't read. If they could read their stuff, they'd stop writing!"
Will Rogers

*I*n no way does the above quote reference any other author. I included it here so I can remember to have fun writing this book . . . and not to take being "An Author" too seriously.

Humor is a subject that I am passionate about, but by no means do I consider myself an expert on the subject. How could anyone think of himself or herself as an expert on humor? Humor belongs to everyone and is there for the taking, if we only choose to do so.

Countless books have been written about humor. They run the gamut from categorized and referenced lists of jokes and anecdotes, to paperback "how to" books for speakers. There are books on the healing power of humor, along with many telling how to develop a sense of humor.

These books are usually well written and full of laughs. Many even refer us to research documenting the great benefits of humor. I must confess I haven't read many of them from cover to cover. Had I known I would someday be writing a book on the subject, I would have read more and paid better attention.

This is definitely not a "how to" book. There's no checklist or any 1-2-3 set of actions to take. You won't find any A,B,C things to do either, for that matter. It is a "why to" book. Hopefully it will persuade you that humor, accepted as an attitude, will simply make your life more enjoyable.

Humor has been around for ages. No one really knows how it originated; maybe with the cavemen. Someone may have stepped into dinosaur dung and generated the first "laugh."

However it originated, humor has evolved with man over the ages and is now an important part of our lives. Hopefully this book will continue the evolution; I'd hate to be known as the person who set humor back 3 million years!

So here's hoping this book meets your expectations, or at least that you can get all the way through it. Given my track record with books, getting all the way through it myself may be a notable accomplishment too. See you at the end!

**"When humor goes, there goes civilization!"
Erma Bombeck**

Warning Label for...Laughter: The Best Medicine

I have heard that "laughter is the best medicine" all my life and am sure you have too. Even if it isn't the "best" by clinical definition, it is definitely good for whatever ails you and is readily available. But it can only be self prescribed.

These days prescription medicines tout their wares and claim their benefits every time you turn on a television. Funny, but every commercial also includes a Medicine Warning Label – a rather lengthy and serious disclaimer describing many unwanted side-effects.

It seems that in our lawsuit-happy society, medicine companies have to name every possible medical scenario in any commercial – some of which actually sound more serious than the ailment the medicine is intended to cure.

The other night, for example, one commercial mentioned "compulsion to drink and gamble" as a possible side-effect. My preacher must be taking that pill; I think I spotted him at the racetrack recently . . . sipping on a martini!

So following their example, I feel it necessary to protect myself from any frivolous lawsuits. That's why I'm including the following Medicine Warning Label. Please read it carefully before using the best universal medicine – LAUGHTER!

Dosage and Administering – The heavier the dose, the better! Refills are always free. Never let a day go by without an injection of humor in your life. It should be self-prescribed.

Over dosage – Heavy usage of this medicine results in joy, smiles and peace of mind.

Medical Interactions – Actually proven to enhance the effectiveness of all other medicines.

Laboratory Tests – Because humans are the only species with a God-given ability to intentionally laugh and spread joy, no testing has been conducted on laboratory rats – only on human "rats"!

For External/Internal Use – Laughter and smiles are for external use, but a keen sense of humor is both external and internal – it is an attitude!

Medicine Withdrawal Symptoms – May include loss of hope, depression, melancholy, worry . . . might make you more difficult to be around.

Precautions

- Can be used if you are pregnant, nursing or plan on becoming pregnant. (It might even expedite the latter!)

- Can be used when driving or operating heavy machinery – if you can manage to see through your tears of joy.

- Not necessary to keep out of the reach of children. In fact, children tolerate and use this medicine more often than adults. We can all learn from them.

- Do not use if you don't want to immediately begin feeling better.

Side Effects

- The neural circuits in your brain begin reverberating. Chemical and electrical impulses start flowing rapidly through your body.

- The pituitary gland is actively stimulated.
- Hormones and endorphins race through your blood.
- Your body temperature rises half a degree.
- Pulse rate and blood pressure increase.
- Your arteries and thoracic muscles contract.
- Vocal chords start to quiver.
- Your face contorts.
- Pressure builds in your lungs.
- Breath bursts from your mouth at nearly 70 miles per hour.
- It is contagious!
- Makes you easier to be around!

If these symptoms persist, you are well on your way to developing a better sense of humor. Even if you've never had one before, there's still hope for you!

Consider yourself warned. You now assume full responsibility for any laughs, smiles and feelings of increased joy. This book might actually have some tangible value. Who would have thunk it?

PART ONE

The Humor Attitude

"The Humor Attitude is the awareness that humor is not just instant gratification produced by laughter but can be a continued state of gratification produced through attitude!"

Jim Bob Solsbery

1

Humor:
The "bologna" of life

"An onion can make people cry but there's never been a vegetable that can make people laugh!"
Will Rogers

Our dog, Miss Lillie, is a red-heeler and poodle cross. Don't ask me how, it just happened. All I can say is, we own her. Let me rephrase that, she owns us.

Miss Lillie is the neatest little dog. She has a long body, short legs, big feet, and poodle hair; along with a red-heeler's intensity and knack for playing ball, catching Frisbees, attacking lawnmowers, and wanting to gain the attention of every cow within hearing distance.

Miss Lillie looks up at me with those big, brown eyes as if to say, "I love you." And I probably go a little overboard, telling her the same. She will do anything for me; but if she ever spots me coming in from the veterinarian's office with a pill she needs to take, she zooms under the china cabinet. So instantly disengaged from the man she will do anything for, he cannot coax her out.

But if I can sneak indoors before she sees the pill, then wrap it up in a piece of bologna, I can hold it out and she'll come running. Like magic, we both get what we want.

So think of humor as the "bologna" of life – easily wrapped

around your communications, relationships, purpose in life, self-esteem and many other thorny challenges. People will come running to you for more, since they are getting what they want. And we might just get what we want too.

I firmly believe that when looking at things through the lens of our Humor Attitude, we can see ourselves, others, and life's challenges more objectively. Doing this can also get us out of a negative thought pattern; and everybody knows that negative thinking solves nothing.

Humor has been shown to be directly related to success. Whether we have a natural, easy-come sense of humor or tend to be a little bit on the stoic side, there is some laughter inside all of us. We just need to make a conscious choice to utilize this God-given gift.

Humor is free and universal, and can immediately boost one's confidence. The quicker we can laugh at something or ourselves, the better off we are – because humor has a way of turning bad situations into good ones.

Why leave something this important to chance? Most of us are always ready for a good laugh, but still go through life waiting for situations and other people to tickle our funny bones. From this point on, you have the universe's permission to become the instigator, finding humor in every aspect of life and then sharing it with others.

> "There are three things which are real – God, human folly, and laughter. The first two are beyond our comprehension so we must do what we can with the third!"
> **John F. Kennedy**

2

Laugh Your Way Out:
Make sure your laughter default mode is set to "out loud"!

"When things aren't going the way we think they should, you just have to Laugh Your Way Out!"
Jim Bob Solsbery

We make conscious choices each and every day, and they determine our happiness. It's not about what happens to us, but rather how we choose to react to it.

My core belief – "humor is more than laughing, it is an attitude" – is a tool I use regularly. Let me demonstrate how this works in moments of stress, which always make us more difficult to be around.

My wife, Jan, and I once attended a conference in Salt Lake City, flying out of Midland, Texas. The flight to Salt Lake City and the return flight were both very trying; but for different reasons.

The flight from Midland went exactly as the airline itinerary said it would. There was no lost luggage, missed connections or late departures. The only problem was that I couldn't adjust to time zones! I thought Utah was two hours later instead of earlier, and two hours different instead of just one.

So I subtracted two hours when converting to Texas time. I calculated our arrival time of 6:10 p.m. as being 4:10 p.m. Texas time. Only five hours of travel time.

To make a long story short, when we departed Midland at 11:00 a.m. and landed in Albuquerque at 11:00 a.m., I knew I needed a lesson in "time zone management." And I discovered that our one-hour layover in Albuquerque had suddenly become four hours. My initial reaction was an angry, "How could I have messed up and ruined our day?"

Now is the time to come clean with you: sometimes my wife has to remind me to practice what I preach, and find the humor in a situation. Her exact words that day were, "We can either be miserable or we can have fun – the choice is YOURS!" It was a nice way of her saying, "If you are going to be grumpy, do it somewhere else and preferably with some-one else!" I got her message loud and clear.

So we ate, shopped, ate again, shopped again and laughed a lot. When the P.A. broadcast the song "It's Five O'clock Somewhere," we took it as an omen to relax in the bar. We were having so much fun we nearly missed our connecting flight. Luckily we didn't, arriving in Salt Lake City at 6:10 p.m. – right on time!

Now for the rest of the story – the trip home. We were sched-uled to leave Salt Lake City at 11:55 a.m. and arrive at Midland at 3:40 p.m. Despite my famous ignorance of time zones, even I knew this was a good schedule!

While waiting in the terminal and having a great visit about our wonderful time in Salt Lake City, we heard the announce-ment, "Flight 2615 to Albuquerque will be slightly delayed."

Later, two more announcements extended the delay, making it crystal clear to me that we'd miss our connecting flight in Albuquerque.

I caught myself feeling irritated; but not wanting to mess up again I told Jan, "Looks like we are in for some more fun on the flight home. Let's just decide right now to 'laugh our way out!'" It was a good thing we made that conscious decision, because the next announcement was, "Would the Solsbery passengers please report to the counter?" Not good.

The gate attendant said, "With new routing, you should be landing at your final destination in Midland at 7:35 p.m. Here's what you do. You will get on your original plane when it gets here but instead of getting off in Albuquerque, just stay on it all the way to Houston. At Houston, change planes and fly to Dallas. At Dallas, you will change planes and fly to Midland. You shouldn't have any problems – piece of cake!" I remember being impressed by his positive demeanor – he had me convinced!

"What about our luggage?" I asked. We were assured our luggage would be re-routed right along with us. Jan and I both laughed out loud. The attendant acted surprised – he'd expected us to be upset.

Two hours late, we finally took off and arrived at Houston at 5:35 p.m. No one had told us we'd have to change terminals and go through security again – we discovered this on our own.

Sweating and out of breath, we reached our gate at 5:50 p.m. and could see our plane, with passengers boarding. Things were looking up! I handed the agent the large stack of tickets we'd accumulated and jubilantly said, "We were afraid we weren't going to make it, but we did!"

She looked at me with a "You've got to be kidding!" expression, tapped on her keyboard and told us, "You WERE confirmed on this flight, but we just gave your seats away. You were NOT on time!" We just stared at each other for what seemed like an eternity. I fought the urge to colorfully explain "Why" we were not on time and where she could put her airplane. Finally, I broke the tension with a broad smile and said, "Okay, what's next?"

As if she had flipped a switch to her "A-game" customer service mode, she smiled and said, "Not to worry, we have another flight to Dallas at 7:05 p.m. Of course you will miss your 7:35 connection to Midland but at least there is a 9:05 flight to Midland. You should reach your final destination at 10:35 – right on time!" I realized her "right on time" was a little different than my "right on time" – seven hours different, to be exact!

The 7:05 flight left at 7:20, giving us time to realize that time does not mean a lot to airlines. Then in Dallas, the 9:05 flight to Midland left at 9:20 (I could see a pattern developing here) and we arrived in Midland at 10:50 p.m. – still laughing and I guess, as far as the airline was concerned, right on time!

On our way to the luggage pick-up, we laughed about the fact there was no way our luggage would be there; and steeled ourselves not to care.

At the baggage carousel, we hung back as other passengers gathered up their belongings. Finally there was just the two of us and an irritated lady watching one lonely, little unclaimed bag going around and around! It wasn't ours or hers; and she was mad. We must have irritated her more by laughing out loud, because she whirled around and snapped, "What is so funny about us not getting our luggage?" I said, "Ma'am, we're just glad WE are here!"

A baggage attendant appeared, got the lady's name and asked her to go to the ticket counter to file lost luggage paperwork. He then asked our name. When I said, "Solsbery," he grinned and said, "We've been wondering where y'all were. Your luggage has been here for hours. It's waiting for you at the ticket counter!"

Flabbergasted, we made our way to the ticket counter and sure enough, there was our luggage. I asked the lady who gave us our bags, "The next time I fly your airline, can I pay for a ticket and then have you tag me as luggage so I could get to my destination on time?"

Unfortunately, some people forget to keep their sense of humor running. Hers must have gone into "sleep" mode, because she wasn't amused.

Having used our sense of humor all day, it was still going strong. Initiate yours during the day, and it generally lasts until bedtime. But I guess we should never assume others will be in the same good mood we are.

We've taken many trips in our lives but have never had any more fun traveling than on this trip. It reaffirmed Maya Angelou's wise statement, "Change the things you can, and change your attitude about the things you can't!"

On the flight out, nothing messed up. It's just that we'd perceived the events a certain way, thanks to my time-zone impairment, and reality took them in a different direction.

Whereas, on the flight home, nothing went as anyone planned – surely the airline never intended for us to circle New Mexico once . . . and Texas twice.

But that day we'd made a conscious decision to be happy, and spent it with other people who'd evidently made a conscious decision to be miserable.

Bottom-line, everyone chooses what type of day they will have. How we react when life isn't giving us what we expect determines how happy we will be. Sometimes you just have to "laugh your way out!"

"The best way to cheer yourself up is to try to cheer somebody else up!"
Mark Twain

3

Humor Facts:
Things that make us
want to say, "Who cares?"

"Analyzing humor is like dissecting a frog.
Few people are interested and the frog dies of it!"
E. B. White

This won't be a feeble attempt to tell you the history of humor, or analyze the intricacies of humor. It will be my equally feeble attempt to share some practical aspects of The Humor Attitude, and some practical ways to bring it to life.

Before becoming an expert on how to write a book – in other words, about 10 days ago – I read that the first step in putting together a book is to write down all your core beliefs, along with what you know of the general public's beliefs about your subject. These could be described as "truisms" or "falsisms" (and if that's not a word, it ought to be – I have a tendency to make up words). The article said to do this exercise in a nice restaurant, where "crowd noise" would stimulate me to think deeper.

Not being a deep thinker I went instead to Taco Bell; and with all the crowd noise (or maybe the Bean Burrito) was inspired to grab a stack of restaurant napkins so I could write down some core beliefs – mine and those expressed by others. Soon 13 napkins were covered with the following thoughts, in no particular order:

Laughter is the Best Medicine: True! Whether or not it's "the best," laughter goes hand-in-hand with what the doctor is trying to do. And it's even free – no co-pay or prescription refills are necessary. Ever.

Funny people never take anything seriously: Absolutely not true! We can, and should, take our job/purpose in life seriously and ourselves lightly. The Humor Project quoted a recent survey of 737 CEO's. Over 98% said they would hire somebody with a good sense of humor over somebody without one.

Some situations are too serious for humor: True! But laughter must be on the program somewhere, and The Humor Attitude is acceptable even in serious times. We must, and will, laugh again!

He who laughs last, laughs loudest: No way! Never let yourself get into "the last word" mentality. As long as laughter is genuine, it makes no difference when it happens.

Having a sense of humor means you're good at telling jokes: Absolutely not true. In fact, many of us need to quit telling jokes. Many "joke tellers" don't exhibit a good humor attitude – and jokes are never acceptable if they're inappropriate in any way.

Laughing on the inside is just as good: Not necessarily (see the next item, too). Some people exhibit very little "outward" signs of good humor, but should smile a bit more! I was giving a speech once and the crowd was rolling in the aisle but there was this one gentleman who never cracked a smile or unfolded his arms. As soon as I was finished, he came up to me and said, "That was the funniest talk I ever heard!" I thought to myself, "Thanks, but you need to tell that to your face."

Laughter is contagious: Absolutely; as proven by a TV laugh track. We've all experienced contagious laughter. So remember to check in with ourselves and make sure our humor "default mode" stays set to "laugh out loud!"

Humor can be disruptive, too: It's sure not as disruptive as being negative, but like anything else, good judgment is always appropriate. I'm a big believer in using humor wisely, and at the right time. Making wisecracks about everything shows a person's insecurity, not their humor attitude.

Funny people are not taken seriously: Unfortunate but sometimes true. For example, my presentations are very humorous but have very deep content as well. Sometimes I don't get hired by event planners who don't think anyone can be humorous and "deep" at the same time. This is not only possible, but very effective. Laughter makes the mind more receptive to communication, and your message becomes easier to remember.

Funny people aren't very smart: Wrong! Whoever came up with this must have been studying me. I can say with great conviction that humorous people are as smart as any, smarter than some, and don't worry much about where they may be on that scale.

Humor is all about laughing: If you have been paying attention to what I said so far, you know my answer to this one. Humor is about more than laughing, it's an attitude! A lot of people consider humor a moment of gratification as fleeting as a laugh. But the truth is, humor will be as deep and meaningful as we let it be.

A sense of humor is natural: It's true, some of us are born with a natural sense of humor that everyone can see – and that's been passed through our genes. But the vast majority of people underestimates their natural sense of humor and never gives it a workout. It's a lot like singing. Almost everyone says, "I can't sing a lick," despite their inborn ability to carry a tune. They convince themselves that to be a singer you have to be trained and ready to sing solos in public; but singing is just singing – in the shower, in church or on stage. Hopefully this book will convince you to not only sing in the shower, but to laugh in there while you're at it.

Humor is impossible for some people: I do not believe this. Everyone has the capacity to find something to laugh about in their life. It's just that some people would rather choose to be impossible.

Humorous people are more pleasant to be around: Well, yeah!!! And isn't that great? I like to say, "Laugh – if not for yourself, for those around you!"

Humor is always a "positive": Humor is a very positive thing – when appropriate. Used in a derogatory way, it becomes negative. Inappropriate humor can be very hurtful and is never acceptable. As a kid who happened to stutter, nothing hurt me more than when people laughed at me. You read that right, this accomplished speaker grew up with a severe stuttering problem. As I'll mention in the next chapter, humor was my number one tool to gain control over my stuttering. This stuff works.

> "A sense of humor is needed armor.
> Joy in one's heart and some laughter on one's
> lips is a sign that the person down deep
> has a pretty good grasp of life!"
> Hugh Sidey

4

Self-deprecating Humor:
Everyone's a joke; some of us just don't get it yet!

**"When we laugh at ourselves first,
it puts us in charge!"**
Jim Bob Solsbery

Before going any further, let's look at one of the most important features of The Humor Attitude – laughing at ourselves.

This is difficult for some people; maybe they don't understand the concept. Laughing at yourself simply means choosing not to take yourself too seriously. There's no better way to build self-confidence than to recognize those moments when we aren't at our best for what they are – proof we're human and not afraid to admit it.

Laughing at ourselves also helps others recognize us as a confident person, with healthy self-esteem.

As my son was growing up, I advised him to laugh at himself. "You are going to do stupid things, we all do. And when you laugh first, you take control of the situation. Then people can laugh with you, instead of at you."

I know the power of this advice, because I used it while growing up with a severe stuttering problem. I mean severe.

I couldn't say my name or put words together in a sentence so they would come out.

You can imagine how other kids laughed every time I got really hung up on a word; but that was just because they were uncomfortable. They didn't know whether to ignore it – which was very hard to do – comment on it, or just laugh from embarrassment because they didn't know how to respond. That's just how kids are.

I remember the first time I laughed at myself before others had a chance to laugh at me. I was about 14 and had gone into town with some friends to hang out in the local drug store. Some girls from a nearby town, about our age, started talking to us. They were very cute as I recall.

When they asked us our names, the other three guys were more than happy to tell them. I didn't say anything. The cutest girl looked at me and said, "Do you have a name?" I think she was flirting with me.

Petrified, I began wishing my parents had just named me Hank. When I started trying to say Jim Bob, you can imagine what came out first. It was, "J-J-J-J-Jim. J-J-J-J-Jim B-B-B-B-B-B. J-J-J-J-Jim B-B-B-B-B-B...Ah heck, just call me Stutterbutt!" I don't know how that last part came out so smoothly, but it did. Everyone laughed; and it was relieved laughter, because I'd taken everybody off the hook.

She said, "You're very funny. I like that." We dated for the rest of that summer – oh, yeah! And that nickname that day stuck through high school. Being "Stutterbutt" didn't bother me, because I'd given myself the nickname. I was in charge!

That was definitely a turning point in my life, because it taught me the importance and effectiveness of laughing at myself. Does humor have any power? What do you think? Now I'm a professional speaker, living my dream of standing in front of crowds of strangers and helping them laugh and become more successful.

**"Against the assault of laughter,
nothing can stand!"**
Mark Twain

5

Jim Bob's Humor Attitude Aptitude Test:
If some people don't know, you can't tell'em

> "The human race has one really effective weapon, and that is laughter!"
> Mark Twain

Before we go any further, let's quantify one important number: our humor quotient. Take this simple test, write down your score for each situation, and then total them up. First, here's the rationale for my scoring system.

We're truly living in the world of "surveys." I spend a good bit of my valuable time taking online surveys for hotels, purchases, service experiences and other items. I also look over my wife's shoulder as she reads magazines that feature personality and relationship surveys. And nearly all of them use the scale of "1 to 5," where "1" is "Strongly Disagree" and "5" means "Strongly Agree!"

I often take the easy way out, checking "3" and taking a neutral position because I don't really understand the question and don't want to appear stupid. The Humor Attitude Aptitude Test is different, so our rating system is too.

Our scale and point values based on the five possible, descriptive answers will be:

1 point – *No way! Not now! Not ever! Leave me alone.*

2 points – *Very seldom, but have been known to do it – before I could stop myself.*

3 points – *Always possible [this answer puts readers in the "neutral, non-controversial" category. Isn't it great being safe?]*

4 points – *Most of the time – if everything else is going right in my life.*

5 points – *Always! Don't care what others think. Just hope they wonder what I am up to!*

Please apply one of descriptions and the applicable point value to the following scenarios:

A. When I pull a bone-headed stunt, I can laugh at myself.

B. I enjoy being around fun people.

C. When the job becomes stressful, I try to lighten the mood for everyone.

D. I have been known to act silly and try to brighten another's day.

E. I am known as a person easy to be around.

F. Family gatherings are more fun if I am there.

G. I consciously look for humor all around me.

H. I love to smile a lot.

I. I love to laugh out loud.

J. The sound of children laughing may be the sweetest sound in the world.

K. I take my purpose in life seriously, and myself not so seriously.

L. I believe a humorous attitude is the main ingredient in being positive.

M. I share humorous stories and cartoons with others.

N. When given the choice of being negative or smiling, I choose smiling.

O. I believe you can't laugh and worry at the same time.

If our score is 66 – 75, our humor attitude will transform itself into a winning attitude. Score of 51 – 65, we are pleasant to be around and have a knack for enjoying life. Score of 36 – 50, we are okay to be around but may have to work on enjoying life. Score of 25 – 35, don't blame others for our spending a lot of time by ourselves – use it to work harder at enjoying life. Score of 15 – 24, time to really work hard on getting a life!

Please be aware that the above evaluation was intended to stress the importance of The Humor Attitude and has no scientific basis. Whatever we scored, it should at least make us think.

"Imagination was given to man to compensate him for what he is not; a sense of humor to console him for what he is!"
Francis Bacon

PART TWO

Using the Humor Attitude in Dealing with Stress, Change and the World in General

"Humorize: To find the absurdity of our reaction to certain situations!"

Jim Bob Solsbery

6

Change:
From Dairy Queen
to Starbucks

**"All change is not growth,
as all movement is not forward!"**
Ellen Glasgow

In Webster's, "humorize" is not listed as a word; so I'm declaring it one here and now. Since I made up the word, it's up to me to give it a definition. The definition of humorize is officially "to find the absurdity of our reaction to certain situations."

When applying the principles of The Humor Attitude, humorizing things becomes very important. Here's how it works.

"Change" is one thing in life we can depend on, and we have to deal with it. So I recommend dealing with it through "humor!"

Before going any further, let me clarify a core belief – that using humor is a conscious decision that should be part of our daily routine. Looking for humor in any situation makes life easier to live.

A little over a year ago, my wife Jan and I decided to move from Big Lake, Texas to Houston so she could build her career in public education. It would also be a great opportunity for me to grow my professional speaking career.

Big Lake is a West Texas town of 2,500, situated at least 70 miles from the nearest Wal-Mart. Having access to a Wal-Mart is a rural "gauge" of "living in the fast lane!"

Another standard is the availability of a Dairy Queen. Big Lake had one and as you might guess it was the town's main restaurant and gathering place. Any time I stopped by the Dairy Queen, I could visit with my neighbors for a spell.

The Dairy Queen was also the "coffee shop" where men liked to gather, drink coffee, and solve the world's problems. Maybe local governments should function out of a small town Dairy Queen – its customers always have the answers!

Once in the Houston area, I couldn't help noticing the shocking lack of any neighborhood Dairy Queens. This means many fewer places where a citizen can exercise the right of every American – the inalienable right of free speech.

I did notice a plethora of Starbucks. They were everywhere – in grocery and Target stores, in malls, in hotels, in strip centers, and free-standing. You couldn't throw a rock without hitting a Starbucks. When we moved into our new house, I first checked to make sure there wasn't one of them in our spare bedroom!

Not only am I not a Starbucks kind of guy – I had never even been in one before. The closest one to Big Lake was 75 miles away; I had driven by it, but was dadgummed sure not going in there. I didn't understand the appeal; and like many people, refused to check out anything new!

After a few mornings of drinking coffee by myself at home, I knew I needed to find a coffee "watering hole" where I could develop friendships and get the day started off right like I had done in Big Lake. The closest Dairy Queen was an hour of rush-hour traffic away, so I decided to check out the nearest Starbucks – right around the corner, of course.

I knew Starbucks was all about coffee, and thought coffee drinkers should be the same everywhere. In 20/20 hindsight, I realize I had not quite grasped a few other subtle differences between Big Lake and Houston. For instance: rural vs. urban, redneck vs. white collar, or town (2500 population) vs. city (3,000,000 population).

But when in Rome, do as the Romans do! So like any self-respecting Houstonian I got into my car to drive about 90 yards, and turned into a Starbucks. There were about 30 people lined up inside, and I assumed my position at the end of the line behind a lot of folks busily talking into their Blueberries, or Blackberries, or whatever berries they are buying these days. I noticed the distinct lack of small talk or neighborly visiting among people in line. Oh well, I thought, I can do something about that.

Unfortunately, after a couple of attempts at small talk I realized nobody wanted to talk to me so I just listened. A few minutes later, I realized I was in over my head – I didn't even know how to order! None of the major coffee investments available to Starbucks clients were on any Dairy Queen menu. By the time I had worked my way about half way to the counter, I was petrified. I didn't want to appear more "ignorant -er" than I already am.

Finally, it was my turn. The counter lady said, "Sir, can I help you?" I just blurted out "COFFEE!!" – I didn't even know if this was a viable order or not. Nobody else had ordered "coffee." She said, "Fine, what size?" I remember thinking "I've got it made – they seem to think I'm one of the locals." Little did I know my troubles were just starting.

I said confidently, "Small." She said, "Sir, we don't have a small coffee." I said, "You DON'T have a small coffee?" She said, "No Sir – Tall is our small." I said, "Great, then give me your small coffee." She said, "SIR, WE don't have a SMALL COFFEE – TALL is our small coffee!" I said, "Fine, then GIVE me your TALL, SMALL coffee!!"

She said, "Whatever" and looked at me like I'd just gotten off the train from Hooterville – at least she got something right. When she brought my coffee I handed over my $9.00 and left! But I only made it as far as the parking lot before they stopped me, so they could get their chair back.

You see, for $9.00 I thought that along with the coffee I'd at least get my choice of one of their chairs.

(Okay, so the chair thing didn't really happen – but you understand my assumption!)

Jan and I had to make the conscious decision to embrace the "change" of a move to Houston. And to embrace "change" means not simply adapting to it. It means seeing it through the eyes of others. If we stay within our own perspective, we never experience the great things that "change" can bring.

We love living in Houston now, because we chose to love living here. Maya Angelou says, "Change the things you can and change your attitude about the things you can't!" (Authors note: My favorite quote, and one that bears repeating.) And we made a conscious decision to use "humor" as our primary agent of positive change.

We shared a laugh about my Starbucks experience, and still laugh about it nearly every day. As we run across other things "new" to us that we're a little hesitant to try, we just look at each other and say, "From Dairy Queen to Starbucks!" This reminds us that we're in for another great experience – if we are just willing to "humorize."

"I put a dollar in one of those change machines. Nothing changed!"
George Carlin

7

Technology:
Passwords and dogs
that I have known

"We are the children of a technological age.
We have found streamlined ways of doing
much of our routine work. Printing is no
longer the only way of reproducing books.
Reading them, however, has not changed!"
Lawrence Clark Powell

I confess to being "technologically challenged." I have come a long way in the last 10 years and have learned to function at a somewhat acceptable level on the computer. At least I can do most of the things I need to, basically handling e-mail and Word documents.

But technology creeps into everything we do, and can get frustrating. At some point I decided that to survive, I had to "humorize" it. The rest of this chapter is from an article I wrote a few years back. Whatever level of technology competence you are at, you will be able to relate to my experience.

A new challenge arose several years ago, as passwords became increasingly important. Doing more and more things "on-line" meant being bombarded with demands for our "User IDs" and "passwords." This trend started out slowly back when I worked for the federal government, and we used the IBM System 36. The biggest challenge was that I could never remember any passwords.

This wasn't too big a problem in the beginning, when passwords were simple four-letter codes we'd change periodically. I could remember them by associating each with a body part or my most recent ailment – simple enough. Thus "cold" or "flue" (sometimes misspell the word to make it work) or just plain "sick," which worked best when a body part was ailing. So after neck surgery I used "neck" and following cataract surgery, "eyes." After wisdom teeth surgery, I used "hurt" because teeth had too many letters. Then there was the password that followed hemorrhoid surgery, which will remain confidential.

Next PCs began to appear at work, complete with Web-based programs. Passwords were a little more complicated, but still manageable. Then came all the on-line databases, and the onslaught of troublesome User ID's. (Ever notice how User IDs are even more difficult to remember than passwords? Sometimes I forgot my User ID, and then knowing my password didn't get me anywhere)

Once the government's affinity for acronyms got mixed with online security, the following issues came on like gangbusters. ("Gangbusters" makes a good password, so make note of it)

Our agency's computer applications were given acronyms: COPS, TACACS, NITC, CAMS, SORS, ADPS, and SCIMS. And the government, in its infinite wisdom, assigned User IDs we could never have come up with on our own! Using my CAMS ID, I reasoned, would work for my SCIMS ID. This might have worked if I could've kept my acronyms straight.

As if keeping up with 15 User IDs and corresponding passwords wasn't enough, they added a list of rules for the length of each password, and what had to be included in it. Oh yeah, I forgot to mention that some had to be changed every 90 days, some every 60 days, some every 30 days, and some not at all. Some had to be 8 characters in length and some had to be 9 or more. The only good news with that was that being able to use more than 4 characters made it possible to use more body parts and illnesses.

By that time a legal-size "yellow sticky" note full of User IDs and passwords was carefully stuck onto my computer screen. Unfortunately, this method didn't work too well. My computer screen was covered, and I was repeatedly told that my giant "sticky" note posed a serious security issue. So, I needed another plan to help me remember my passwords.

Many years earlier (before I started using body parts and illnesses as my four-letter passwords) the name of my dog, Spot, was my first password. What a brilliant plan – use the names of my dogs as passwords! Nobody can forget his or her dog's name, right?

I have a Heel-a-poo (red heeler-poodle cross) named Miss Lillie, so WHAM, in she went as a password. That was followed by two more dog names, Twister and Choco. I also used the name of my neighbor's mongrel, Chaos.

I was off and running – never to have a problem with passwords ever again! My system worked great until somebody decided we needed new passwords. These passwords had to be changed and couldn't be reused; and some passwords had to include numbers and even special characters like @, #, $, %, or &.

There was only one solution: get some more dogs! Along came Tiger, Sandbagger, Spike, Buster, Puddles, Dadgummit, Slickwillie, Beauracrat, Twospots, Threespots, Fourspots, and Nospots. Nospots was solid black; after 90 days when it was time to change my password he became Blackie. After another ninety days he was Charcoal. Then he was . . . gone. I went outside one night to call that mixed-up mutt home, and he never showed up. Must have suffered from an "identity crisis."

Then we were told to include a number, so Twospots, Threespots, and Fourspots became 2Spots 3Spots, and 4Spots. It didn't make any difference to them, they still came when called.

Before long, disaster struck in the form of a new rule stating that passwords had to be 9 characters in length. They had to include two numerics, two special characters, and two capitalized letters. This was the last dog I ever got. I named her M9Z4!228?. She was a sweet dog but she never did learn her name. And sad to say, she was never petted. Maybe that's because I couldn't remember her name, so of course I avoided calling her.

When I decided to retire, I began to find good homes for all of my dogs. It worked out fine, and we are now down to two dogs – Miss Lillie and M9Z4!288? Miss Lillie was our first, so she had to stay, plus she and I enjoy eating chocolate chip cookies and Blue Bell Ice Cream together. I couldn't break up a team like that!

And I'm happy to report that M9Z4!228? will come running to me anytime I say a cuss word. She's been spending a lot of time in my lap lately – mostly when I am at the computer trying to keep up with the torrent of User IDs and passwords I now have to use with accounts at banks, credit cards, utilities, on-line retail accounts, on-line bill paying, and my government retirement account.

I've decided against using any dog names in the future. I'm too old to exercise any more dogs. I have reverted back to the big, yellow "sticky" on my screen. It still works and never needs to be walked!

"It has become appallingly obvious that our technology has exceeded our humanity!"
Albert Einstein

8

Politics:
We have the best government that money can buy

"What I value more than all
things is good humor!"
Thomas Jefferson

I wish I could leave this chapter out of my book. But if
there was ever a group of people who need to take their
purpose in life more seriously and take themselves more
lightly, it is politicians.

Especially politicians on the national stage. This doesn't
mean that state and local elected officials get a "get out of jail
free" card – although this would come in handy for many of
them. I still have a reasonable amount of confidence in most
of them. I just hope they don't blow it by doing something
too stupid!

We are now in the middle of the 2008 election cycle – in
itself, a very depressing spectacle. Let me say up front that I
am an independent who leans toward the conservative side
of things. Don't hold that against me and I won't hold your
"leanings" against you.

There is nothing wrong with people having a difference of
opinion. In fact, it is healthy. If the entire population believed
exactly as I did, we would probably even get less accom-

plished than we do now, because there would be no new ideas and no good debate. And also, it would appear that the way I believe is the only way to do things. This perspective makes it unnecessary to look at any new ways to solve challenges; after all, I am already getting my way.

Does this sound familiar? This "my way is the only way and if you have a difference of opinion, you are somehow a mis-informed moron – or worse" mindset is almost as irritating as it is prevalent in Washington today.

I respect differences in opinion. I respect someone standing on their principles. I respect party platforms. I respect per-suasive debate. What bothers me is when members of either political party vote only along party lines. This tells me they can't think for themselves. I do not believe that a Democrat or a Republican, elected by their constituents to represent them in Washington, was sent there by the voters to let party leaders dictate every decision.

We elected them because we hoped, and prayed, that they would collectively solve the challenges facing us every day. Boy, were we wrong!

Washington politics is in gridlock. Politicians there should remember they are not any smarter than the rest of us. They just happen to be in a position to vote "yay" or "nay" thoughtfully, in an attempt to make things better. And that's what they should do. In the words of Nike, "Just do it!" Or maybe Larry the Cable Guy said it best, "Get'er done!"

This morning I read that the House of Representatives passed a resolution, 402-3, proclaiming a certain day 'Frank Sinatra Day.' It was actually passed 7 days after the specified date. They couldn't even get that done on time, and with all but three agreeing on it. Turns out the three who voted against it were just protesting that Congress has more important things to consider. There may be a ray of hope for these three.

Even though this book is loaded with humor and is an excellent opportunity for members of Congress to "laugh at themselves," I'll bet most of them wouldn't take advantage of it. If "What I value more than all things is good humor" was good enough for Thomas Jefferson, it ought to be good enough for today's elected leaders. They need to wrap their serious purpose in the humor attitude by smiling more, caring more, listening more, and doing more.

Actually, the reason I wrote this chapter was to try and help the general public somehow make the situation more tolerable by "humorizing" politics. Believe me; it helps us digest the evening news.

I do not like cynicism and I know I am sounding cynical. I challenge the politicians to give me a reason to sound otherwise. "Mr. Politician, the American people have never needed you more than they do now."

"Humor is the best antidote for the politician's occupational disease: an inflated, overweening, suffocating sense of self-importance!"
Mo Udall

9

Stress:
You can't laugh and worry at the same time

"Usually, we can handle stress with a large dollop of common sense, an ability to see things as they really are, and with humor to bring back your perspective when you've blown things out of proportion!"
Loretta LaRoche

Stress is just non-productive worrying; and I firmly believe that you can't laugh and worry at the same time. So, problem solved!

I know, it's not really that easy. But we can deal effectively with stress. This is probably the one area of our lives where we have the most control over; because, for the most part, it is not the events in our lives but our reaction to those events that cause stress.

Quoting Maya Angelou again, "Change the things you can and change your attitude about the things you can't!" I try to live by this mantra everyday. It is framed and on my desk where I can see it during the course of the day.

While no "expert" on stress, I do have a fairly deep understanding of it – and not because I'm a psychologist or have studied it and know all of the answers. It's because I study myself and I know what "stresses" me. The true answer is, "I stress me!" It's my humanness (I wasn't sure that was a word, but spell-check signed off on it anyway).

Unless you have three eyes, four legs, six arms, a tail, and breathe through a different orifice on your body, you're human too! That means you will have stress and various things will happen to you – guaranteed!

Some people complain, "Why does everything happen to me? Things never happen to others like they do me." In this "poor me" attitude, we are an open invitation to more stress.

We may be saying, "But Jim Bob, aren't there things in life we have to take seriously? Are you suggesting we can laugh every stressful moment away?" There are two answers to those questions: 1) "Yes" and 2) "Absolutely not!"

We all will have serious issues and events in our lives. By the Grace of God, we will get through them. This is not the kind of stress I am talking about. Most stress comes from our reaction to things that really don't mean a damn thing (excuse me for cursing, but it got your attention).

Here's an example from this week, when I was in Target at the pharmacy counter picking up a prescription. A lady in front of me was also there to pick up a prescription she had called in earlier that morning.

The pharmacist couldn't find it. The lady said, "WELL, it had better be here. I called it in early so I wouldn't have to wait!" The pharmacist apologized and said, "If you will give me just 5 minutes, I will fill yours now. If you have any other shopping to do in the store, feel free to do so." The lady said, "My time is valuable. I am so upset I am going to change pharmacies!"

The pharmacist said, "We value your business and please allow me to show our appreciation by giving your prescription top priority right now." The lady wouldn't let it go. She said, "Only because my time is important and it would take up a lot more of my time to get this filled somewhere else." She then continued to tell him every other customer service complaint that she had that day in this store and others. I thought I was seeing a pattern developing as to why she was so unhappy: her choice of attitude.

I noticed by my watch that she had been berating the pharmacist for 9 minutes. Remember the first thing the pharmacist told her was that he could fill her prescription in five minutes. Finally she let the pharmacist go and she turned and looked at me. I was grinning.

She said, "That would irritate you too, wouldn't it?" I said, "No, it would not. Five more minutes is not going to ruin my day." She looked as if I'd insulted her intelligence. At least she was right on this point. I wish I could tell you that my Humor Attitude somehow became manifested in her and she repented and left there a happier person. Unfortunately, that didn't happen.

Before the five minutes was up, the pharmacist returned with her prescription, took her $5 co-pay and she stormed off – stressed and unhappy. If she could have simply changed her initial reaction, not only would she have been out of there ten minutes earlier, she would have left there much less stressed!

And, oh yeah – I had more shopping to do and when I checked out 20 minutes later, there she was with a shopping cart full of other items. She saw me and immediately went to another check-out line – a line that was longer and going to take up even more of her precious time.

I thought about how sad it was that she'd chosen to ruin her day. We all have a tendency to do this – maybe not as arrogantly as this woman, but to some degree.

Experiencing stress in our lives is 100% guaranteed. Will we control it, or let it control us? There's no better way to control stress than seeing it through the eyes of humor.

I know when I "humorize" a stressful situation; the stressful feeling is often replaced with a feeling of acceptance. It doesn't seem as serious anymore, which is probably because it was never that serious to begin with.

A study by Dr. William Fry found that a 5-year old laughs more than 200 times a day, while adults laugh 5 times a day or less! As we grow up, we are told to be serious and then we start applying this to everything in life. We suffer from "hyperseriousness." Spell-check didn't like this word so I looked in Webster's and sure enough, I have made up another word. And you know my rule. If we make up a word, we have got to give it a definition. So my definition of hyperseriousness is "the tendency to make life too difficult."

I like to talk about how we choose to make life too difficult, which leads to a plethora of excuses as to why we can't have fun right now. We say things like, "I can't laugh now. I don't have time. Maybe I can laugh on Saturday. I have 2:00 available on Saturday. I will laugh then." And then Saturday gets here and something else gets in the way and guess what, laughter is put off until later . . . and "later" never comes.

I wish I had a dime for every time someone comes up after my speech and says, "I laughed until my face hurt" or "my sides are sore from laughing." My answer is, "Take that laughter with you and use it daily. Apply it to life!"

Wouldn't you agree that stress comes primarily from exaggerating the seriousness of an event? Humor is powerful enough to defuse these exaggerations; and then BOOM – we have laughter! And in dealing with stress, laughter is our goal. You just have to Laugh Your Way Out!

"The greatest weapon against stress is our ability to choose one thought over another."
William James

10

Aging:
My knees buckle but my belt won't

"None are so old as those who have outlived enthusiasm!"
Henry David Thoreau

George Burns said, "You can't help getting older, but you can help getting old." Aging is a subject on which everyone is an expert, because it affects everyone. I hear people in their 30's and 40's complaining about aging. I'm glad I am aging, because I'm not too fond of the alternative.

I don't know when we first become labeled a Senior Citizen. I'm not sure the label "Senior Citizen" really means anything outside of some monetary discounts. And companies aren't even consistent on this issue.

AARP sends us their invitation to join when we turn 50. IHOP lets you order off of their Senior Citizen menu at 55. At other restaurants, it's 60 or 65. I saw an offer the other day that said, "Discounts offered for those 70 or over!" It was probably for something like surfboards, roller blades, or cell phone texting; I know it wasn't for hearing aids.

So I'm confused. When do I become the proverbial Senior Citizen? The cliché, "You're only as old as you feel" came to mind but it really is not that relevant either. So I developed a test along the lines of Jeff Foxworthy's "You are a redneck if…" to help me put aging in perspective.

You are a Senior Citizen if….

… your knees buckle but your belt won't!

… you have more hair in your ears and nose than on your head!

… your favorite game is "Sag – you're it!"

… you've still got it . . . but nobody wants to see it!

… you start making the same noises as your coffee pot!

… an "all nighter" means not having to get up and go to the bathroom!

… brain cells come and brain cells go but fat cells live forever!

… you have first hand knowledge that you shouldn't take a sleeping pill and laxative on the same night!

Do you get my point? We only become old when we quit finding the humor in aging. It is all about our mindset. How do we view aging? Like everything else in life, I choose to view it with humor. If there was ever a stage in our lives when we need to laugh at ourselves, it's when we become preoccupied with aging.

The key is not to become preoccupied with aging, or its aches and pains. Of course they are real. Putting items in a place where you will be sure to find them and then looking for them hours on end because you can't remember the place is also real. It happens to everybody. Laugh about it!

My dad lived to be 85, and he loved to laugh. He exemplified The Humor Attitude long before I coined the phrase, but I knew he had it. He was fortunate to have lived a relatively healthy life. Then a few months before he passed away, doctors discovered he had cancer.

I was sitting with him in the hospital about two weeks before he passed away. He was having a good day and we were having a good visit. The nurses had come in to give him a sponge bath, shave him, and comb his hair. He had false teeth and the nurse offered to clean them for him.

He took the teeth out and handed them to her; she brushed them and gave them back to him. After she'd left he said, "If you have ever brushed anyone else's teeth, you might be a redneck!" Then he looked at me, smiled, and said, "Once an adult, twice a child." My dad never lost his sense of humor or fantastic attitude.

My goal in life is the same as his. Keep the humor level up, the attitude positive and your Humor Attitude fully engaged at all times. I remember how his humor that day made me feel better, and how I needed it. You see, humor is not just for us. It is also for those around us and those who love us.

No one likes to watch their parents or loved ones being slowed down by aging. I didn't and I'm sure my son won't either, but what helped me the most is that my parents didn't gripe or complain. They knew their positive attitude and sense of humor also benefited the family. I'm selfish enough to appreciate that.

I plan on keeping this in mind so I can age more gracefully. Humor will benefit me – and hopefully keep my wife from electing to "stop" my aging process, if you get what I mean.

And of course it will benefit our son and his family. They'll have enough to deal with in their lives without having to humor a grumpy old coot! And wouldn't it be great for them, after I am gone, if their memories of me are of the times my sense of humor helped them to feel better – not all of the times I complained about getting older.

"Always go to other people's funerals, otherwise they won't come to yours!"
Yogi Berra

PART THREE

Using the Humor Attitude to Enhance Self-improvement

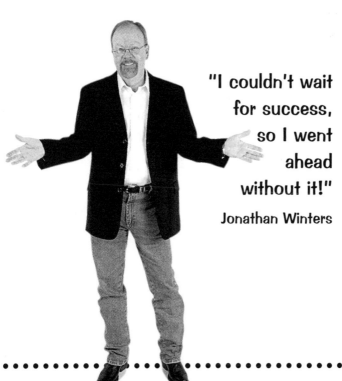

"I couldn't wait
for success,
so I went
ahead
without it!"

Jonathan Winters

11

Life Balance:
Had I known I was going to live this long, I would've taken better care of myself

"Just as your car runs more smoothly and requires less energy to go faster and farther when the wheels are in perfect alignment, you perform better when you thoughts, feelings, emotions, goals, and values are in balance!"

Brian Tracy

We hear so much today about life balance. It's almost as if it has just been invented. The truth is, it's been around forever but we called it "common sense." And many of us have had a tendency to push it to the back burner. For that reason alone, I think it's worth a chapter in this book. Or in anybody's book, for that matter.

I believe in having a life balance. We need to stop what keeps us busy and think about our lives. Is there a proper balance? Is there any balance? If not, we're missing a great opportunity to be more, do more, and enjoy life more.

Humor is one of the best "lenses" through which we can look at our lives. It helps keep everything in proper perspective, and even see how absurd our priorities are.

Remember that word I made up – humorize? Its definition is "to find the absurdity of our reaction to certain situations!" If we apply this to life balance, it helps us keep it simple!

You've probably figured out by now that I am really a pretty simple guy. We have a tendency to over-analyze as we search for the "meaning of life" – whatever that means. Let me give you a simple way to look at your life balance situation.

Think of life as a big checkbook. In presentations I tell my audiences to imagine receiving a checkbook with $10,000 in their account. The money is theirs to spend at their discretion. Everyone agrees to spend their money. Naturally, some will spend it faster than others; but eventually all will spend it. The accounts will become empty and for those who spend it faster than a roadrunner through a carwash, their accounts will probably become overdrawn.

Life is the same way. If all we do is debit against our life account, then we will become empty and even worse, overdrawn. We have to make deposits along the way. And we make deposits into our life account by finding time to do the things we enjoy, especially by spending time with family and friends whose company we enjoy.

We also make deposits by tending to our spiritual life; by laughing more and by injecting "positives" into our attitude; by living a healthy lifestyle that includes exercise and weight management. We make deposits by giving value to others, and by giving value to ourselves. And when we do this, we can maintain a positive balance in the "checkbook of life."

And if we wrap our approach to life in The Humor Attitude, it isn't really that overwhelming, is it? I can hear some of you grumbling out there, "Jim Bob, with my job, it's not that easy. How do I balance work and pleasure when my job is so miserable?"

Donald Trump said, "If you're interested in 'balancing' work and pleasure, stop trying to balance them. Instead make your work more pleasurable."

One of my presentations is called, "Bring your best person to work – each and every day!" I talk about coming to work more energized, more enthusiastic, more positive, and with a smile on our face. If we can act like we want to be there, our jobs become easier and more pleasurable! And we will also be more productive.

The key is to talk to ourselves. How many of you talk to yourself? How many of you just thought, "I don't talk to myself." We all talk to ourselves. Just don't forget to ask, "What am I telling myself?"

Is our self-talk a constant negative barrage, or the expression of our belief that we can make things more positive? There's nothing more powerful than the mindset we talk ourselves into (pardon the preposition at the end of the sentence, but sometimes it just makes more sense).

Having a positive mindset and bringing your best self to work goes hand in hand. Before you know it, your life will be moving in more positive cycles.

You may have noticed I haven't told you much about myself yet. So here it is. I'm "rural" – a fancy word for "country." I grew up at Maryneal, Texas, a sleepy little town with a store, a church, a post office, one road in and one road out. I talk about it a lot in my speeches because the life lessons I learned there while growing up still apply today.

One lesson I speak about is based on an elderly couple who lived there in a very tiny house. They barely got by – they actually farmed a very small garden with a mule.

Everyone called him "Manana" Robertson because he was a procrastinator. He got his nickname because you could ask him, "Can you come help me?" and he would always answer, "Maybe manana!" (Spanish for "tomorrow").

His wife had to nag him to prepare their garden every year. She would say, "Percy" – that was his real name – "Percy, hook up that mule and plow the garden!" "Percy, hook up the mule and PLOW the garden!" "PERCY, hook up the mule and plow the garden!"

This would go on for days until finally Manana would say, "Today's the day. I'll hook up that mule and plow the garden!" He went out this one particular year and the mule had died the night before.

She said, "Percy, what are we going to do? What are we going to eat? Had you gone out the first eight days I told you to go, at least we would have a garden this year – and we would have a whole year to get another mule. I can't take it anymore. You put things off and you never tend to business. I've had enough. I'm through!"

Manana said, "Woman, I've had enough! You hook me up to that plow and I'LL PULL IT!" They used a leather harness to hook him up to their little one row, wooden plow, and sure enough he actually started pulling it.

It had rained the day before, so Maryneal's sandy clay loam soil was soft enough for the plow to actually turn the soil. As he kept on plugging Percy would look back, and saw that the row was 10 feet long and getting straighter. He kept on plugging! He looked back and saw that the row was 20 feet and even straighter. He kept on plugging! He was smiling – she was smiling! Thirty feet – 40 feet – 50 feet and now he was plugging faster.

Then 80 feet and 100 feet – he reached the end of the row but just kept going. He hit the barbed wire fence, rolled through the barrow ditch, and wound up lying in the middle of the road.

She threw the reins down, climbed the fence, and ran over to where he lay. "Oh Percy," she said, "Are you alright?" He said, "Woman, don't you know how to say 'WHOA'!"

There is no better way to make a deposit into our "checkbook of life" than knowing when to say "Whoa!" – to regroup, rethink, relax and rededicate. And to take time to enjoy the humor opportunities that life brings us each and every day.

Then we can not only bring our best self to work, but bring our best self back home at the end of the day. And when this happens, a proper life balance is within reach.

> **"I believe that being successful means having a balance of success stories across the many areas of your life. You can't truly be considered successful in your business life if your home life is in shambles!"**
> **Zig Ziglar**

12

Dieting:
If diet food tasted like chocolate, we would all be skinny

"I do not like broccoli. And I haven't liked it since
I was a little kid and my mother made me eat it.
And I'm President of the United States and I'm not
going to eat any more broccoli!"
George H. W. Bush

This book is sounding more and more like a self-help
book, rather than a humor book. Hmmm! Maybe the two
go hand in hand. Come to think of it, it also reads a lot like a
life balance book. Maybe the three go hand in hand in hand.

I wasn't sure I would include this chapter. It really didn't
fit into the scheme of things (as if this book has a cohesive
theme). On the other hand, it is about a subject with which
probably 90% of the population deals. A day doesn't go by
that I don't hear someone say "I'm on a diet," "I need to go
on a diet," "I hate diets," or "I hate people who don't have to
diet!" And that includes yours truly.

A lot of those folks don't talk about having to diet, but just do
it in a non-verbal, unobtrusive manner, staying aware of the
food they're putting into their mouths, and the words coming out of their mouths.

The number one rule for dieting should be, "Don't talk about it all of the time, just do it!" Or if we do talk about it, at least demonstrate your Humor Attitude.

After all, it's humorous that there are as many different diets as there are hairs on my head. That would be anywhere from 6 to 106 depending on the light – or lack thereof. It is so easy to get confused from all the choices; and for some of us, the amount of confusion equals the amount of food being consumed.

Maybe you can relate. I have been on a diet, then switched to another diet and finally added another diet . . . only to realize when I switched; I didn't stop the other diets. I was eating the food recommended by all three!

And how about those fad diets? They may have merit but never worked. For instance the diet many years ago where you ate 10 prunes each day. It didn't work, but my wife always knew where to find me.

I also will never forget the "7 Day Diet." I went on it, and quickly lost a week!

Why do we fall for any diet published in a magazine or book? It's as if because something is in print, by golly it must be true! If my book doesn't accomplish anything else, it should prove that something getting printed does not necessarily mean it has great literary value.

I could go on and on about diets. The Grapefruit Diet, the Banana Diet, the Low Carb Diet, the High Carb Diet, the High Protein Diet, the Low Protein Diet, and the Eating Standing on Your Head diet! If that isn't one, it will be some day; remember you heard it here first.

Needing to lose weight and maintain a healthy body is no joking matter. It has been proven beyond a shadow of a doubt, that healthy eating adds years and quality to our lives. But at some point, we are probably going to mess up with our diet. Instead of beating ourselves up and saying "Pass the biscuits and gravy," we need to call upon humor to help us.

I'll write down all the foods that give me a problem saying no to. Then I'll give every food on the list a humorous name and begin referring to these foods by their new names.

This doesn't necessarily need to be done out loud. Just saying them to ourselves is fine, and will reduce the noise level too. But the key is to not eat a bite of these foods unless we can identify them first by our secret "term of endearment."

These terms might include:
Chocolate becomes *Chunky Cheeks*...
French Fries becomes *Belly Buster*...
Ice Cream becomes *Butt Builder*...
Biscuits & Gravy becomes *Thunder Thighs*...
Beer becomes *Beer Belly*...(How original)
Chips & Dip become *Fat Fusion*...
Cheesecake becomes *Silent Cellulite*...

Always using such terms helps us stay aware of consequences; and the key to dieting is probably awareness of what we are putting into our mouths. If we do this, we'll never look at these foods again without our brains triggering the unpleasant association. If a strong visualization kicks in, we might just curb that craving. By the way, why is it that we never crave broccoli?

We all know people who can eat chocolate and never gain a pound. I'm still trying to decide whether to hate them or envy them. And there are those disciplined enough to eat 100% right, 100% of the time. Those folks, of course, are probably too disciplined to be reading a book of this quality. But if this describes you and you did buy this book, count your blessings...and feel free to skip to the next chapter because you may not be perfect at everything.

There's no better way to feel better about ourselves than by eating healthy and looking better. Do I do it all of the time? Who does? But with the help of a little common sense, I probably eat healthy 90% of the time. I did lose 50 pounds eight years ago and manage to keep it off.

The main thing I do is to remember this simple yet proven formula:

If calories burned exceed calories taken in,
then weight loss occurs.

And I remember that it takes a balance of common sense, proper nutrition and activity...and yes, vigorous laughing is an activity. I even read somewhere that if you can laugh for 10-15 minutes a day; you'll burn enough calories to lose over 4 pounds a year!

"There is one thing I have never taught my body how to do and that is to figure out at 6 A.M. what it wants to eat at 6 P.M.!"
Erma Bombeck

13

Communication:
I know I'm talking,
I recognize my voice!

"Courage is what it takes to stand up and speak; courage is also what it takes to sit down and listen!"
Winston Churchill

I've read that the first two minutes in a conversation are the most important. I agree, because I firmly believe people have to like you before they will ever hear what you say. Humor is a great "bridge" to accomplish this. Victor Borge said, "A smile is the shortest distance between two people!" A smile can also be a universal language; so smile early and often.

I'm no expert on communication, but I do know a little about how it works. After all, I've been a professional speaker for over 25 years and am pretty certain that the spoken word is one of the major components in verbal communication. But don't forget to listen too!

I don't see a lot of difference in the spoken word or the written word. The writer also needs to grab my attention and make me care about them to keep me reading. A little humor usually serves me well.

Both forms of communication are effective and the mechanics are similar. I speak my words to myself as I write this book, and hope you are doing the same as you read this book. The main difference between reading and listening is that you can read this book in the bathroom and we can continue to communicate. Thank goodness, I don't see that happening a lot in my speeches!

And there is more. Most communication experts agree that 60% of communication is non-verbal. Body language, facial expressions, action and reaction can be very powerful.

The Humor Attitude is just as important in non-verbal communication. Think about Jack Benny, who was much funnier when you could see him. Younger readers think about Tim Allen; the same is true with him.

Quality communications should be a priority in every facet of our life. Jan and I knew a married couple living in our small town. One day, the man and I were talking about his communication skills, and he told me he'd signed up for a communication seminar on the next Saturday, in a city about 100 miles away.

He got up early on Saturday morning, had breakfast with his wife, and then ran by the office before leaving town. He arrived at the seminar just as it began. He walked in to take his seat and there, right in front of him, sat his wife. They had each signed up for a "communication" seminar and driven 100 miles in separate vehicles, without knowing the other was going. That's funny!

Advertisers effectively use the written or spoken word so you'll like them and buy their product. They also use a lot of video, audio, graphics and other non-verbal tools. All of them use humor when it is a good fit for their product. Of course, humor would not fit with all products any more than it fits in every situation.

Before writing this book, I watched a lot of television to look for humor in advertising and discovered that approximately 60-70% of commercials used humor, or at least kept their tone "light."

Consider Super Bowl commercials. They're so popular, even non-football fans watch and comment on them. Almost every Super Bowl commercial is humorous, but advertisers don't use that much humor just to be named "best of show," even though this is quite a coup. They use it to make you remember their company and like their product.

Humor is a powerful tool for making a message more "likeable." I went to a Dallas Cowboy's game several years ago. Despite all the pageantry and hubbub, I most vividly remember one vendor whom we saw hawking corn dogs up and down the aisles.

He was chanting, "Get your hot corny dogs right here! Get your hot corny dogs right here!" One new customer yelled back at him, "Hey, these are cold!" The vendor never missed a beat. He smiled and just started a new pitch: "Get your cold corny dogs right here! Get your cold corny dogs right here!"

Our group was so impressed with his quick humor, we stopped him on his way back down and each bought a corn dog. Yeah, they were cold but we didn't mind. His humor had made him likable, which made us want to hear what he had to say and to buy what he was selling.

The Humor Attitude is very important as we communicate our way through life. We need to wrap it around our words, our non-verbal actions and our personality. We need to smile more, be pleasant, give value to others and don't be confrontational. Just like the Miss Lillie story, we may find that people come running – and they get what they want and we may get what we want.

"It was impossible to get a conversation going, everybody was talking too much!"
Yogi Berra

14

Self-motivation:
I feel more like I do now than I did a while ago

"People often say that motivation doesn't last.
Well, neither does bathing – that's why we
recommend it daily!"
Zig Ziglar

Success in any part of our lives builds confidence in all other areas. The best way to get motivated is to focus on what we do well, and find ways to do more of what works for us.

This is true even with activities such as weight loss, exercising, or improving your appearance. Eight years ago I lost 50 pounds, and couldn't believe how it boosted my confidence and enthusiasm for getting more accomplished. And it should come as no surprise that the Humor Attitude played an important role in my transformation.

Have you ever heard the saying, "The clothes make the person"? I read in today's paper about a study (there being a study for everything) in which researchers took tiny, drab birds and used a cheap marker to darken the rust colored breast feathers of the male barn swallow.

Evidently, having darker colored breast feathers is the way male barn swallows prefer to look. The study revealed that this more attractive appearance triggered changes to the birds' body chemistry, which increased testosterone. The birds seemed to feel better about themselves because they were more attractive to the female birds. Well, duh!

The researchers aren't sure how this testosterone boost happens; what matters is how the little guys felt better about themselves. I suspect they were not only making some feathers fly in their relationships, but also became better "early bird worm getters" too!

(By the way, do you think these researchers got in any trouble with their mothers? It reminds me of the time I spray painted our tan cat and made him a black cat. I thought he looked better but apparently the cat and my mother did not agree.)

The point is we do feel better about ourselves and can become more self-motivated with even the simplest improvements. You'll be able to relate to something I finally accomplished this week for the first time in my life. It involved those "punch cards" that offer something free at the carwash, laundry, sandwich shop or somewhere after ten purchases.

I'd gathered these for years with the best intentions, but after one or two punches would always lose the card (which may have been what the retailers had been counting on). I tried to keep them organized but when I took one into the sandwich shop they'd tell me, "This is your carwash card" and vice versa. And I couldn't even remember to accumulate the "single punched" cards until they all added up to 10 punches.

Well, this week I was cleaning the debris out of my car (so I could go to the carwash and get another new card started) and I hit pay dirt. I noticed several of these cards strewn about . . . and they were mostly from one place, the dry cleaners.

My heart was racing with anticipation as I gathered them up and started to count. They totaled three punches... then five...then six. I found two cards over the visor and this brought my total to eight. Then I spotted one peeking out from under the floor mat...that made nine! I frantically searched for one more but to no avail.

After two hours of fruitless searching (although I did find the electric bill from four months earlier that I'd sworn to my wife I had mailed), I was almost ready to question the meaning of my life, given this serious failure. Then on my way back into the house, I noticed a piece of paper in the bottom of the dog's food bowl. I reached in and pulled out a gravy soaked punch card. My heart was pounding as I turned it over...sure enough; it was from the dry cleaners!

Jubilantly, I raced to the dry cleaners, where they pointed out that my little stack of cards had no value unless I had something to be dry cleaned. But so what – I'd assembled enough holes to get something free! Like a little barn swallow, I left the dry cleaners with my chest out, chin held high and feeling better about myself.

We can build on our successes in life, large or small. Let them set the positive attitude we need to motivate ourselves to succeed again and again.

And don't let others tell us what is wrong with us. Have you been to the bookstore lately and walked down the self-improvement aisle? I never knew I had so many things wrong with me! Self-help books can be helpful, unless we spend so much time thinking about what's wrong with us; we lose focus on what is right with us.

The key to self-motivation is self-motion. Start moving in the right direction and take it one success at a time to avoid feeling overwhelmed. And remember, sometimes you just have to "Laugh Your Way Out!"

"Always bear in mind that your own resolution to succeed is more important than any other!"
Abraham Lincoln

15

Leadership:
I'm their leader!
Which way did they go?

"A sense of humor is part of the art of leadership, of getting along with people, of getting things done!"
Dwight D. Eisenhower

As a speaker who teaches leadership skills and techniques, I could list the traits of an effective leader… but I won't. Instead, I'll talk about one of them, The Humor Attitude. It is definitely beneficial for leaders and one I put pretty high on the list when doing leadership training.

Many think "humor" and "leadership" are a conflict of terms. Thinking about the effective leaders in my life, the one common denominator was that I liked and respected them. Some other leaders may have achieved some success, but I didn't like and respect them and none of them could "lead me" to want to do my best.

A few other "leaders" didn't know when to be serious, and joked their way through life. I rarely liked or respected them either. Still others tried to lead by intimidation, cracking the whip all the time without giving value to others. Maybe you can guess how much I liked and respected those folks.

But the leaders who took their purpose in life more seriously than they took themselves were truly effective. I liked and respected them and wanted to be a part of their success.

I wrote down the names of a few well known leaders who have gained my respect, and probably would have my loyalty if I'd been directly involved with them. In no particular order, they are:

Winston Churchill   Vince Lombardi
Franklin Delano Roosevelt   Thomas Jefferson
Martin Luther King Jr.   George Washington
Ronald Reagan   Abraham Lincoln

This group achieved a lot, and definitely affected many people for the better. I suspect they probably used a pretty good balance of humor in their leadership approach.

Most of us can remember Ronald Reagan and his humor. During the Presidential campaign in 1980, Reagan's age became an issue to some. He was 70 years old, and Walter Mondale used this against Reagan. It worked until one of the debates.

During that debate Reagan said, "I will not make age an issue of this campaign. I am not going to exploit, for any political purposes, my opponent's youth and inexperience." Reagan's age, almost overnight, became a non-issue.

Reagan's ability to use humor and poke fun at himself was a large part of his being called, "The Great Communicator." He really knew how to use it even during some serious situations. After being shot by John Hinckley, Jr., Nancy rushed with him to the hospital. The first thing he said to her was, "Honey, I forgot to duck." He asked the doctor, "Are you a Republican?" I remember how his humor helped the nation during this trying time.

I almost put Moses on that list, because surely he had a sense of humor. Can you imagine being given the job of leading your followers to the Promised Land and being lost for 40 years? There must have been times when he used humor to diffuse the situation. Surely, he took ribbing because he, like all men, would not stop and ask for directions.

Some business leaders have been very successful and used humor to optimize their results. The founder of Southwest Airlines, Herb Kelleher, built the most successful airline in history based upon his employees and his customers having fun.

If you have ever flown Southwest Airlines, you probably have a story of humor being used by the crew. They do it a lot, and it has never failed to make me feel better...even when I am in the last group to board.

Everyone is a leader at some time or another. Leadership does not come with being CEO of a Fortune 500 company, a military commander or a boss. The synonym for "to lead" is "to guide." At some point in all of our lives, we are asked to give guidance and should all want to be the best leader possible.

Humor and The Humor Attitude definitely have a place in leadership. They help put people in a better mood; and people in a better mood are generally more accepting, more productive and more cooperative. If the people we lead accept our vision and they like and respect us, we'll successfully reach our desired destination. Just ask Moses!

"If a leader can make their work more fun, then they can lead others to do the same!"
Jim Bob Solsbery

PART FOUR

Using the Humor Attitude in Relationships

"I never
met a man I
didn't like!"

Will Rogers

16

Family:
You can pick your nose but you can't pick your family

"A happy family is but an earlier heaven!"
George Bernard Shaw

I was wondering how to start this chapter when I decided to take a lunch break. Over my sandwich I began watching a re-run of Home Improvement, and Tim the Tool Man gave me my inspiration.

In the show, his son Brad wanted to go snow skiing with friends over Christmas. Jill, the mom, wouldn't hear of it. She wanted the entire family home for the holidays. Of course, Brad, being the proverbial 13 year old, did not understand how they could show such a lack of understanding.

Brad's argument was, "All my friends are going and it will be a lot of fun." Tim was trying to reason with him. He said, "Brad...Christmas is not about being around people you like. It's about being around family!"

We can all relate to what Tim said. There's not a more trying time than holidays as we are hurrying about traveling, cooking, and trying to fit visits into a short period of time. The stress doesn't come from the fact that we don't like the family members we are visiting. It comes from the pressure we feel to visit.

This is a good time to break out The Humor Attitude; and

because it is family, the humor is built in if we look for it. Be the leader and break out the games or just do something to lighten up the situation for everyone.

I know a lot of pictures are being taken. If it's Christmas, everybody, including the kids, will either have a digital camera or just got one as a gift. It looks like the paparazzi just arrived on the scene. So try this next time you have a family get together. Print out several pictures, especially the candid ones, and organize a "caption contest."

Try not to use the posed shots of everyone standing in front of the Christmas tree with forced smiles, or if it's Easter, of everyone stiffly posed in their Easter best. Look for those candid shots where people have their mouths open and there is not any food going into it.

Caption contests are a blast and you will be surprised how funny they can be. You can think of some very funny things that Aunt Esther might be saying to Uncle Hubert in that picture where she's talking to him, he's in the recliner with his eyes closed, and he has unbuckled his belt because he ate too much dressing. This obviously works at family reunions as well.

Speaking of family reunions, the Solsbery bi-decade family reunion is coming up soon and I'll be there as usual. The Solsberys' don't gather very often and when we do, it's not for very long. Don't be late because we eat lunch early, belch, take a short nap and leave. Visiting is optional. A lot of the fun comes from the fact that we've changed somewhat in five years and we won't recognize each other.

For this reunion, I'm going to do something similar to Jeff Foxworthy's, "You might be a redneck if...." jokes. It might go something like this:

- If you only recognize half of the people at your family reunion, you might be a Solsbery.

- If you think seeing cousins once every five years is adequate, you might be a Solsbery.

- If you have ever attended the wrong family reunion and didn't know the difference, you might be a Solsbery.

- If you take a lawn chair that converts into a cot for your nap, you might be a Solsbery.

- If you can squeeze five years worth of visiting into two hours, you might be a Solsbery.

- If you had a great time at the family reunion and can't wait to do it again in five years, you might be a Solsbery.

Consider doing one of these for your family, too. A lot of the fun is to do it as a group during the reunion or particular holiday visit. Just remind everybody to lighten up and not take it personal. Make sure the humor is something that would appeal to the whole group.

Family is built around love and acceptance...love for each other and the memories we cherish together. And, acceptance of the fact we have all changed and moved on in life. Yes, visiting with family is important but don't lose sight of the fact that during visits, "quality" will most always trump "quantity."

Be the one to "qualitize" (there I go again, making up a word) the visit with humor and laughter.

"If we open a quarrel between past and present, we shall find that we have lost the future!"
Winston Churchill

17

Marriage:
I have found the secret to a happy marriage – I don't try to run her life...and I don't try to run mine!

"I have learned that only two things are necessary to keep one's wife happy. First, let her think she's having her own way. And second, let her have it!"
Lyndon B. Johnson

I have used humor most of my life and I knew it played an important role in enjoying life. But sitting down and focusing on it long enough to write a book has amazed even me. For every chapter, I have the tendency to say that this will be the area where humor is truly critical. This chapter on marriage is no exception.

I'm proud to have a wonderful marriage. I give 50% of the credit to Jan, my wife, for her commitment and understanding as to what it takes to make a marriage work and I give the other 50% credit to her for her ability to use humor in putting up with me. She makes me laugh, she makes me smile, and she makes life fun. And all of this without any talent in telling a joke!

Some of you out there are whining and saying, "I can't tell a joke so therefore I can't use humor!" I hope by now you are starting to get the philosophy of The Humor Attitude. I say it again, Jan cannot tell a joke but she exudes The Humor Attitude.

She loves to laugh and thank God she can laugh at my goofy humor. She has a sweet smile and a loving, caring spirit about her. She truly loves me and lets me know it daily. She's fun to be around and doesn't have a phony bone in her body. She makes me feel special.

We love to laugh together. Our favorite TV shows are comedies and we literally make each other laugh out loud. Let me go on the record right now and recommend that you and your spouse make it a point to laugh out loud together.

Jan and I have "humor triggers" we have collected over the years. These short phrases are used a lot, and as soon as one of us says one of them, it lightens whatever subject is at hand.

Some of these triggers come from times that maybe had a little tension in them. Or maybe they came from one of us getting our words tangled and something coming out wrong. They are not funny to anybody else. In fact, they rarely make sense to anybody but us. These "humor triggers" work beautifully. They always seem to put things in the right perspective for both of us.

Let's face it. Married people spend a heck of a lot of time together and we just can't leave having fun to chance. It has to be a priority. If you need to review the chapter on "Self-deprecating Humor," do so now because this is a "must" in marriage. There aren't many faux pas' we can hide from our spouses. They know us, blemishes and all.

Speaking of blemishes, we might as well move into the bedroom with our discussion, because it's also a priority in marriage. I don't know why I just didn't entitle this chapter "Sex." Well, actually I do know why. My wife told me I shouldn't write about something that I didn't know much about. I have always looked at sex kind of like golf – you don't have to be good at it to enjoy it!

One favorite old joke I use on occasion (to the right audience) is told as if it actually happened to me. It goes something like this…I was asked to give a talk for a woman's club luncheon when their scheduled speaker had to suddenly cancel. This particular club met monthly and always had a speaker come in and talk about such topics as How to Exercise Without Breaking a Sweat, Lose 10 Pounds in 10 Days, Does Your Husband Find You Sexy?, 10 Complete Meals Under 100 Calories, Fluid Retention, and other subject matters of interest to women.

Knowing this, I asked what the topic was to be for the program. The President of the Club said, "Well, it was 'The Importance of Sex in Marriage' but we certainly wouldn't expect you to do that!" I told her I thought I could handle the subject – might even be able to add the man's perspective.

I was telling Jan about the upcoming luncheon and when she asked what the topic was to be, for some reason I didn't feel comfortable telling her so I said "sail boating."

I gave the talk and it went very well. The ladies were very polite, even laughing at my stupid jokes and occasionally nodding as if I might have gotten a few things right.

The next day, one of the ladies in attendance who knew my wife ran into Jan at the grocery store. The lady said, "We certainly did enjoy Jim Bob's talk at the luncheon yesterday. He was very entertaining and seemed to know quite a lot about his subject." Jan said, "I don't know how! He's only done it twice – the first time made him sick at his stomach and the second time his hat blew off!"

I do feel comfortable writing this chapter because I do know a lot about the bedroom! I know how many different colors I have painted it during the past 10 years, what 10% of the closet is mine, the fact that the dog is Jan's bed partner of choice and takes precedence, that having 12 pillows on the bed does not mean I can use one of them to sleep on, and why a dust ruffle is required. Actually, I'm not sure about the dust ruffle. I just know not having one is not an option.

There's no better place to practice self-deprecating humor than the bedroom. Be ready to laugh at yourself and the many faux pas' that will invariably happen. And guys lose that macho mentality – you're not anywhere close to the blond, shirtless, six-pack ab hunk on the cover of the romance novel that your wife reads. Be okay with it! You are her slightly balding, looks-better-in-a-shirt, one-pack paunch choice of a man and if you are doing your job right, she is more than okay with you!

And men, as you laugh and make fun of your aging body you will endear yourself to her BUT if you don't remember anything else in this book, remember this – DO NOT, I repeat DO NOT laugh and make fun of hers. Even when she asks, "Am I getting fat? Do you see any cellulite? Are my breasts still perky?" Just look her in the eye and unequivocally say, "No way...Not a bit...Heck yeah!" That's your story and you're sticking to it!

As I write, it's the day before our 26th Anniversary. We're going on a date and will have some great laughs. And if any jokes are told, I'll have to tell them and Jan will politely laugh, whether they are funny or not!

"I have great hopes that we shall love each other all our lives as much as if we had never married at all!"

Lord Byron

18

Raising Children:
My wife says our son must have gotten his brains from me...she still has hers

"Do you know what you call those who use towels
and never wash them, eat meals and never do
the dishes, sit in rooms they never clean, and are
entertained till they drop? If you have just answered,
"A house guest," you're wrong because I have just
described my kids!"
Erma Bombeck

Jan and I are fortunate that our son, Cade, was such a good kid. He never gave us any trouble and we're thankful for that. But, challenge or not, we tried to do our best.

You have to admit, the way we raise our children now is a lot different than the way we were probably raised. I feel today's society can go overboard when it comes to recognition of any type of achievement.

Cade was a very sharp kid and received many accolades for his academic achievements and leadership qualities. He deserved every one of them. But Cade, bless his heart, got his athletic ability from me – which certainly didn't make him a star athlete. When I was in high school, I overheard my coach say, "Jim Bob has deceptive speed. He's slower than he looks!"

Cade, being a smart kid, figured this out on his own. When he delivered his Valedictorian speech, he challenged his classmates to focus on their strengths. He said, "I cannot be the next Tiger Woods, but Tiger Woods cannot be the next Cade Solsbery either."

And now he is grown, married to a wonderful girl named Megan, and they are about to make us grandparents for the first time. When I update this book, you can bet it is going to have a big chapter on grandkids. I've already picked out my grandparent name. I'm going to be "Gramps!" Jan said, "I hope it doesn't turn into Grumps."

If our son was such a good kid, why am I telling you to use The Humor Attitude to enhance the raising of kids? Because humor is important in not only the trying times of raising kids, but in their everyday development. We can help our children develop a positive sense of humor, and we can reinforce them when they exhibit appropriate humor.

We were big on the appropriate part. It is easy for kids to get caught up in the "laughing at the expense of others" mentality. Kids easily succumb to peer pressure and want to be thought of as cool by the "cool kids."

And many times, kids use laughter to deal with certain situations and the laughter is not always appropriate and often hurts other kids. They mimic the actions of others, and they for sure mimic the actions and attitudes of their parents.

We have no greater responsibility than being proper roles model for our children and this includes the appropriate use of humor. If we laugh and make fun of others, don't you think our kids will do the same?

As kids grow up, it is also a great time to reinforce the importance of laughing at themselves – those times when they pull a bonehead stunt and know other kids are going to ridicule them.

I referenced my own experience with this in a previous chapter and how it helped me in my overcoming my stuttering. What I didn't say in that chapter is how my mom and dad helped me to not take myself so seriously. They are the reason I had the courage to laugh at my stuttering before others laughed at it.

Having said all of that, kids are a great source of humor, especially the little ones. If you are not keeping a journal of the funny things your kids do and say, start now. It will serve as great entertainment when the kids are grown and will also come in handy if you ever want to blackmail them.

When Cade was about five years old we took him to the pediatrician. Jan thought he was constipated and wondered what to do about it. The doctor told us, "A lot of times, kids are just too busy playing to take the time to go to the bathroom. Just make sure Cade spends some time each day sitting on the toilet, reading a book while he sits there (I always wondered where this habit came from!) and this will help train his body to function properly."

We didn't even know Cade was paying attention. The next day, we missed him. We finally found him sitting in the bathroom on the toilet with all lids down, all his clothes in place, and reading a book. When we asked what he was doing he gleefully responded, "Just doing what the doctor said!"

I don't know why that reminded me of one of my favorite jokes. A two-year old had swallowed a bullet. The mother rushed him to the doctor. The doctor examined him thoroughly and said, "He should be fine. I'm going to give you this laxative to give him when you get home...just remember not to point him at anybody."

We can learn a lot from the natural joy of children. The little ones love to laugh, don't they? When I graduated from college, I taught school for two years at a little rural school. I also drove a school bus and if I live to be 100, I will never forget a little six-year old boy who rode my bus. He never shut up. He sat right behind me and yacked in my ear every morning and then every afternoon.

One day, he laughed out loud in my ear. I said, "Everett, don't do that!" He said, "I'm sorry sir. I was smiling and it busted!" That's what happens to smiles – they bust!

**"I think Little League is wonderful.
It keeps the kids out of the house!"**
Yogi Berra

19

The Work Environment:
I don't have a clue when work starts here...it's already underway when I show up

"The brain is a wonderful organ; it starts working the moment you get up in the morning and does not stop until you get into the office!"
Robert Frost

In most jobs, we spend more time with our co-workers than we do our spouse. If you don't have a spouse, just play along!

The major difference is we choose our spouse. Unless you are the person in charge of hiring, you did not choose your co-workers. And even when you are in charge of hiring, the Forrest Gump Factor, "You never know what you're going to get," can always kick in.

The chapter that was to follow this one was going to be entitled, "Dealing with Difficult People." I decided to lump it in with this chapter. I am in no way saying that all people we work with are difficult, but let's be honest, some are. There is nothing better than The Humor Attitude when dealing with these people.

I don't know about you, but when I spend 8-10 hours each day with other people, I want it to be as enjoyable as possible. Humor is a great way to enhance not only your mindset, but the mindset of the workplace as well. And mindset, better known as attitude, is everything when it comes to making work more enjoyable.

Please try this exercise. Write down the top 10 things that irritate you at work. You might want to do this on a separate sheet of paper. If you write them in the margins, at least be careful to whom you loan this book, they might be on your top 10 list.

Now review the list carefully and ask yourself this question, "Can I change this?" If you can, then problem solved. If you can't (and most of your top 10 will fall into this category), then just change your reaction to it. Remember the Maya Angelou quote I keep on my desk and have use multiple times in this book, "Change the things you can and change your attitude about the things you can't!"? Is this doable? Absolutely! I do it all of the time.

There will always be people who don't "get it" and never will. I feel sorry for them, because they make themselves miserable. And intentionally or not, they do their best to make you miserable as well. They were probably on your top 10 list, right? But more importantly, did anyone put you on their top 10 list?

Loretta LaRoche is a psychologist who's written many books and gives many programs on stress. She is one funny lady, and a big believer in the use of humor to put things in the proper perspective. In one presentation she talks about those people at work that set out to not only ruin their day, but to ruin other's as well.

She uses an example of someone who's having a bad day and whines, "This is a horrible day. I can't get anything done today. Every time I start making progress, something interrupts me and I just have something else to deal with. I've been so busy today; I haven't even had time to go to the bathroom!"

When we have a good day, and we all do, why don't we say, "This is a great day! Everything went as planned. I've gotten a lot done today. I've been to the bathroom six times. I could have gone more but I didn't need to!"

How we express ourselves to others is very important, and can set the tone for the entire day for everyone. We definitely have an influence on our work environment – whether it is negative or positive is up to us.

How we express our expectations is just as important. One definition of work is "to achieve an objective or result." I'm not the brightest bulb on the tree but I suspect you were hired to do just this so it should be your priority. And when the work environment is productive, everyone feels better about themselves so people are more likely to want to become a team member.

And negative expectations are just as infectious. As a senior in high school, I was on the football team. We weren't very good that season. We only had one substitute and we never won a game. Our coach never expressed any positive expectations of our performance. In fact, I don't think he had expectations of us at all; and somehow we felt this.

His pre-game pep-talks lacked the "pep" part (say that six times real fast). We were always apt to hear, "If we kick off, block the extra point" or "If we receive, recover the fumble."

To enjoy work more, raise your expectations of what you can accomplish. And it doesn't hurt to raise the expectations of those around you at the same time.

You've got to "humorize" a lot of things at work. In case you've forgotten, my definition of humorize is "to find the absurdity in our reaction to certain situations." Sometimes our perception of what work should be is the most absurd part of our day.

Webster's definition of work included words such as labor, travail, toil, drudgery, and grind. Let's come up with our own definition of work – one that's more realistic and positive. My definition of work is:

"A place where I show up to do what is asked of me and they pay me and then I can go home to loved ones and enjoy the necessities of life and enjoy the extra's in life that money can bring and take my kids on vacation and laugh a lot and watch my kids grow up and put my kids through college and laugh a lot and be romantic with my spouse and retire someday and laugh a lot and enjoy traveling and visiting with grandkids and then look back with thanks that I had a job to make all of this possible!"

We are going to work, at a job or for ourselves, for most of our lives. Be clear on the rewards of doing so and on what our life would be if we were unemployed or out of business. Which vision is more powerful?

My most powerful vision is what life would be like without a fulfilling job, or the determination to build a successful business. I expect the same is true for you.

Our job is what we make it! Make it more fun and be glad to have one. If you don't have a job, keep the faith and your sense of humor…you will find one.

"Men, for the sake of getting a living, forget to live!"
Margaret Fuller

PART FIVE

Using the Humor Attitude in Difficult Times

"It is a common experience that a problem difficult at night is resolved in the morning after the committee of sleep has worked on it!"

John Steinbeck

20

Tragedy:
I must laugh again...someday!

"The mark of your ignorance is the depth of your belief in injustice and tragedy. What the caterpillar calls the end of the world, the Master calls the butterfly!"
Richard Bach

Hopefully you're finding this book somewhat humorous and a fun read. I know I've thoroughly enjoyed writing it.

As an avid believer in The Humor Attitude and the benefits of humor, I feel compelled to include this part on how to use them in difficult times. It's probably not going to include funny stories, but it will tell you how humor has helped me get through rough times. And the key to rough times is to get through them. Winston Churchill said, "If you are going through hell, keep going!"

Most of the next chapters are about me and my personal experiences or thoughts. I'm not a psychologist and will not be telling you how to deal with your tragedies and grief. I will never say to those who have lost a loved one or suffered other kinds of tragedy, "I know how you feel." I don't know how they feel. I know they are hurting; but we all handle things differently.

A few weeks after hurricane Katrina, I was speaking at a luncheon for a large Chamber of Commerce in east Texas. We had a great time and the crowd was rolling in the aisle. They laughed a lot as I told them about The Humor Attitude and the importance of finding humor in all situations.

When I finished, a young lady reporter from the local TV station said she would like to interview me for their evening newscast. I remember thinking to myself, "Boy, I must have been good. They want to put me on TV and tell the world!"

After the crowd cleared, I met her and a cameraman at the back of the room. They didn't waste any time getting started. The cameraman hit me with a very bright light as she stuck the microphone in my face. With an angry tone she demanded, "How can you expect the victims of hurricane Katrina to laugh in the face of tragedy?"

Needless to say, she caught me off guard. For a moment I was speechless. It seemed like an eternity, but was probably only a few seconds. Then I gathered my composure, smiled into the camera and said, "I do know if they do not laugh again, they will not survive." Her anger subsided and we continued on with what turned into a great interview.

She'd interpreted what I had said in the speech to mean we should immediately find humor in everything, and can solve anything just by laughing. That was not what I was saying then . . . and not what I am saying now.

Bad things happen to all people. It's called life. And I know there's a time to laugh and a time to cry. I do not believe that everything in life can immediately be laughed away, but I do believe humor can smooth out bumps in the road of life. After all, humor and laughter are a gift from God, given to us for a reason. They can play a very big part in the grieving and healing process.

I only had one sibling. My sister Jaylene probably exemplified The Humor Attitude better than anyone I have ever known. She loved, she laughed (a lot), and she made those around her feel special.

I received a call one day at work from my niece, who told me that my sister Nene (my childhood name for her) had been rushed to the hospital and was in intensive care. I dropped what I was doing and drove the 100 miles in a relatively short period of time.

Nene was only 59 and had not been sick very much in her life. Yet over the course of the next 93 days, all in intensive care, we watched as organs began to shut down and she slowly passed away. They never really discovered what was wrong with her.

During those 93 days, I spent a lot of time at the hospital with her husband, Bill, her son, Tam and her daughter, Christi. This tragedy played out over time – too long a time. There was crying but also laughter. There had to be. We could not have lasted 93 days without it.

Some tragedies occur suddenly, while others play out over time. Humor has a different role depending on the circumstances. For instance, we will never forget 9-11. This national tragedy for everyone was a personal tragedy for many.

I'll never forget how I felt that morning as we watched the live news coverage. The whole world watched and was affected. We all had to deal with it as best we could. I remember clearly being told to leave work and on my way home, stopping by the grocery store to buy a half-gallon of Blue Bell Ice Cream. I guess I wanted comfort food. I don't really remember eating it but by bedtime, it was all gone.

And over the course of the next week, I remember watching a lot of re-runs of the Andy Griffith show. Humor served as an escape from reality. Some might say, "This is not good," but it was for me. I watched plenty of news about the event and what followed but at times I needed a break.

There was no humor in the event. There never will be. But as I looked back during the weeks following 9-11, I found humor in the fact that my first reaction was to buy ice cream. Mark Twain said, "Against the assault of laughter, nothing can stand!"

Be it hurricane Katrina or 9-11 or watching a beautiful, wonderful woman wither away over 93 days, there is no "quick fix" to make the hurt go away. But I do know that if we do not laugh again, we will not survive.

"Tragedy is a tool for the living to gain wisdom, not a guide by which to live!"
Robert Kennedy

21

Illness:
If laughter is not the best medicine, it is dadgummed sure the cheapest

**"The secret of learning to be sick is this:
Illness doesn't make you less of what you were.
You are still you!"**

Tony Snow

If you recall, there was a warning statement at the front of this book for laughter, the best medicine. This was a humorous attempt to mock medicine television ads, but there's a lot of truth in it too. If we can utilize humor when we're sick, it can expedite the healing process.

If nothing else, humor and The Humor Attitude create a positive, more carefree mindset; and a positive attitude helps us deal with illness.

Illness is a broad term, covering anything from the "sniffles" to a life threatening disease. I've been very fortunate to this point in my life not to have had any serious illness; but many friends and family members haven't been as fortunate. Maybe you've had a serious illness or have one right now.

Worry is natural for anyone suffering from serious illness, but that doesn't mean we should not or cannot reduce our worrying. As someone said, "You can't laugh and worry at the same time!" Even if laughter only gives our mind and body relief for a short time, it is definitely worth it.

Have you ever been around a children's hospital? The emphasis is on bright colors, fun things to do, humorous videos, and other things that help the kids be more cheerful. Even clowns are used on a regular basis. It may or may not help with the "healing" part but it sure helps with the "dealing" part.

I would like to see more of this in all kinds of hospitals. No one is in a hospital because they want to be and they are sure not there for the food. If you can't find humor any other way in a hospital, at least find it in the food.

Recently, my best friend, Cuppy Graham, was in the hospital for an extended stay. From his bed he liked to announce his "Name the mystery meat contest." Did this make him well? No. Did it make him feel better? Yes. It made all of us feel better, because for a while humor was lifting our spirits.

As caregivers of loved ones who are ill, we want to do more. I remember caring for my dad, my mom and my sister, and the feeling of helplessness it brought with it. But I could always give them a smile, and most of the time they gave it back to me. For one brief moment, we'd all feel better.

Sometimes we just need to let folks know that we "believe." The lighter our mood, the more confidence and hope we'll be able to share with people who need it the most. It's hard to be hopeful if we can't be cheerful, so try and cheer each other up whenever you can.

If I ever have a serious illness, I hope to have the positive attitude of my best friend Cuppy Graham. For three years he never lost his sense of humor, although at times it was very difficult for him. But he "lightened" many moments for all of us and hopefully we did the same for him.

His wife, Betty Anne, was a great caregiver. Not long before he passed away, they were discussing details of his memorial service. Cuppy and I loved good country artists who sang old songs; artists like George Jones or Ray Price.

We'd become serious fans of a young Texas singer named Jake Hooker, so Cuppy's son had arranged for Jake to sing at Cuppy's memorial service. Betty Anne thought Cuppy would want to know this so she told him. Cuppy simply smiled and said, "Dang, I wish I was going to be there."

Even at such a serious moment, Cuppy and Betty Anne managed to laugh out loud. Did humor and laughter heal Cuppy? No. Did it help him cope with his illness? Yes. Did it lengthen his time here on this earth? I definitely believe it did. Did it give him more quality time? Absolutely!

New medical marvels are announced almost every day, and new cures are being discovered as we speak. What would have been terminal a few years ago is now considered a manageable illness. If you or a loved one is going through an illness, just keep the faith, harbor hope, hang in there and look for new things to laugh about.

As someone once reminded us, "When you've lost the will to laugh, you have lost the will to live."

**"I enjoy convalescence. It is the part
that makes the illness worthwhile!"
George Bernard Shaw**

22

Loss of Material Things:
The stock market didn't break me...I had all of my money tied up in debt

"Success is going from failure to failure without a loss of enthusiasm!"
Winston Churchill

In many speeches I talk about Maryneal, Texas – the sleepy little town where I grew up. I also talk a lot about life lessons I learned growing up on a ranch, around working cowboys. My dad was a rancher and cowboy. It is all he ever did in his life and he loved everything about it.

Ranchers make a living with things they can't control... weather and market prices, for example. This makes them great at taking things the way they are, and leaving those results they can't control to the Man above.

Audiences enjoy hearing my story about what happened to us during a seven-year drought in the 1950's. A lot of ranchers didn't come through that drought in good financial shape, I tell them. "But my dad was a good rancher. He didn't go broke in 1956 like everybody else. He saw it coming and went broke in 1954."

There's actually some truth in that. In the middle of the drought, my dad liquidated his herd and took his losses early. Had he tried to hang on, he would have lost even more money.

Droughts can be devastating, so I admire the ranchers' spirit. They kept their sense of humor up and running. I'm sure my dad was very concerned but never let it show.

Many ranchers got a chuckle over blaming the local weatherman, who everybody called Chicken. No "weather predictor" or meteorologist, he just tracked rainfall amounts and turned the data over to the National Weather Service. Chicken was quite the jokester himself.

One hot, dusty, dry afternoon at Check's Barber Shop in Roscoe, Chicken blurted out, "I am betting that it NEVER rains again." The farmers and ranchers said, "Chicken, that's the dumbest thing we ever heard." Chicken said, "I don't know about that. Five people have already paid off!"

Everybody had a good laugh as they left to drive back to their dusty, parched ranches. They felt better about the future thanks to Chicken's humorous way of reminding them that the drought would end and that life would go on. And of course, that was one forecast he got right.

After the drought, my dad borrowed some money to restock his ranch. Things really turned around, but he couldn't resist reminding me, "The grass is green. The cows are fat. The cattle prices are good. This is a good opportunity to get ready for the next drought."

That was not a negative statement that contradicted the Law of Attraction. It was simply a statement of the obvious – droughts are inevitable. Its message that tough times are inevitable was one we all should keep in mind.

Whatever you do in life, there will be bumps in the road; we'd better learn to laugh about it. I have lost jobs and businesses, material things and money. But I never lost my sense of humor.

Like everyone, I got down at times. Getting back up every time is the key to success. Henry Ford went bankrupt seven times while trying to start Ford Motor Company. When asked about his failure in inventing the light bulb, Thomas Edison said, "I have not failed. I've just found 10,000 ways that won't work."

Those ranchers in Maryneal prepared for the next drought, even in the middle of a rainstorm. And they knew rain was coming eventually, even during a drought. Their experiences gave them plenty of common sense.

William James said, "Common sense and a sense of humor are the same thing, moving at different speeds. A sense of humor is just common sense, dancing."

The ranchers at Maryneal taught me many life lessons, but none were more important than to keep looking upward – to the skies for rain, and to God for guidance and comfort. They kept it real and they kept it simple – and more importantly, they kept it humorous.

"The worst thing that happens to you may be the best thing for you if you don't let it get the best of you!"
Will Rogers

23

Challenges:
"Just be patient sir,
he'll get it out in a minute!"

"It is our attitude at the beginning of a difficult task which, more than anything else, will affect its successful outcome!"
William James

By now you should know how strongly I believe in the power of humor and The Humor Attitude. Here's the number one example of how it helped me successfully deal with a major challenge in my life.

I already mentioned earlier my severe childhood stuttering problem, which made it impossible to even say my name. Forget about putting words together in a sentence. I wouldn't answer the telephone, because even a simple "hello" just wasn't there.

Let's take a brief pause to "chase a rabbit," as we said on the ranch. Have any of you ever lived on a "party line?" As my crowd gets younger, I have to explain the meaning of party line! It's where people share the same telephone line. Everybody's phone had a different ring, so you'd know a call was for you.

One lady on our party line was named Gladys, and Gladys liked to carefully monitor each and every incoming and outgoing call, so to speak. She of course knew about my stutter.

I was at home by myself one day when the telephone rang, which scared me to death because I had to answer; if it was Mom and Dad and I didn't answer, they would be worried. Our ring was one long ring and four short rings. The phone rang again – one long and four short. My heart stopped beating. Fear gripped me!

I heard another one long ring and four short rings and started for the phone...my heart pounding. Another one long, four short – I was saying the word "Hello" over and over in my mind, willing it to just come out. Another one long, four short – I was getting closer. Another one long, four short – I picked up the phone and said, "Heh...Heh...Hehh...Heh...!"

The gentleman on the other end of the line was trying to get the conversation started. "Hello. Hello. Hello. Hell-oooo!" But I could only repeat, "Heh...Hehh...Heh!" Suddenly I heard Gladys helpfully chime in from her own phone, "Just be patient sir, he'll get it out in a minute!"

To return to my main story: this was a very challenging time for me. I attended Highland, a small rural school with one long hall. The first grade was on one end, and high school on the other. The recommended curriculum plan in those days was, "Start down here in first grade and try to graduate out the far end in 12 years."

Yes, it was a simpler time, but my teachers played a monumental role in my life. They loved me, they hugged me and probably at times, stepped out in the hall and cried a few tears for me. They knew how much the stuttering upset me. Combined with their support, my God-given sense of humor is what enabled me to deal with my stuttering every day.

My six classmates and I eventually made it all the way down the hall to high school. I'll never forget my English teacher, Elmore Alexander. One day in class he said, "Jim Bob, it's time for that oral book report!" He knew how I hated speaking to the class but said, "Get on up there. You'll do fine!"

Twenty minutes later I finally finished my five-minute oral book report, exhausted and sweating. My six classmates were tired and sweating, too . . . as well as Mr. Alexander. He was happy to let me go back to my seat and regain my composure. Then in a few minutes he walked over to my chair, put his hand on my shoulder and looked down at me. "Jim Bob," he said, "you've got what it takes. You're going to make an after-dinner speaker someday!"

I thought the man was crazy! But if Mr. Alexander said it, he meant it! I knew he'd seen something that I didn't see in myself. That day he planted a dream of becoming a public speaker, a speaker able to help people laugh with me, instead of at me.

After Highland I went to Texas A & M University, where I had to find a job. Finally, I answered an ad in the Austin American Statesman and got a job selling Bibles door-to-door. I received my kit and the first week, I sold 121 Bibles. The second week, I sold 118 Bibles and the third week, I sold 123 Bibles!!!

The president of the company called me and said, "Mr. Solsbery, we don't know what you are doing but you are doing it right. You have broken all records in only three weeks selling Bibles and we want to bring you to Austin, our corporate headquarters, so you can tell us how you sell Bibles and we can break our company's national sales records."

I didn't want to go, but he offered me $75 so off I went to Austin, and was soon standing in front of some 300 people. He introduced me as "Jim Bob Solsbery – a freshman at Texas A & M University, who has broken all our records in his first 3 weeks. Now he's going to tell us how he sells Bibles!"

I got up and said, "W-w-well, I w-w-walk up to the door and when the lady answers the door, I say 'Hi M-M-M-Mam! My name is J-J-J-Jim! J-J-Jim B-B-B-B-Bob. Jim B-Bob Solsb-b-b-b – Jim B-B-B-Bob Solsb-b-b-bery!!!! I sell B-B-Bi-Bi-Bi…I sell B-B-B-Bib-Bib…I sell B-Bi-Bi-Bib-BIBLES and do you want to buy one, or do you want me to read it to you?!'"

Here's a disclaimer, which I never thought I would have to use. I told this story one night at a banquet and on the way out, a little lady grabbed me and took both of my arms. Looking up into my eyes, tears running down both of her cheeks, she said, "God bless you son for selling all those Bibles!" I thought, "My gosh, they're starting to believe all this stuff!"

The stuttering problem was true, the party line story was true, and the Mr. Alexander story was true, but folks, here's the truth: I never sold any Bibles.

You'll probably hear that story at my presentations. It is always a crowd pleaser and I don't tell it to make fun of my stuttering, or your stuttering, or anyone else's speech impediment or handicap. But it's about who I am and where I came from, and shows the power of humor, the power of perseverance, and the power of an encouraging hand!

"The best things in life are usually difficult!"
Dirk Benedict

EPILOGUE

"If we couldn't laugh, we would all go insane!"
Jimmy Buffet

I was looking for a way to end this book without giving you whiplash, sort of tying it all together. I noticed some books had "epilogues" and wasn't sure what an epilogue was, so I looked it up in Webster's.

Webster's defines it as a concluding section that rounds out the design of a literary work. Even though this book does not – in any shape, form or fashion – meet the criteria of a literary masterpiece, it does loosely fit into the category of a "literary work." So please accept this summary and update as my epilogue.

A lot has happened since I wrote the first draft of this "literary work" some six months ago. I contemplated rewriting some chapters, but decided just to update things in closing.

Our son Cade and daughter-in-law Megan indeed gave us our first grandchild – let me rephrase that – gave us our first "grandchildren!" They were in their fifth month of pregnancy when during their second sonogram the doctor exclaimed, "I see two!"

The earlier sonogram had missed one because of a rare type of pregnancy called Mono-Mono. The babies were in the same amniotic sac and therefore, in the early months had appeared to be one. Cade and Megan were in shock as they were told of the high risk of her being able to carry the babies until the 32nd week of pregnancy – this being the most optimistic goal of the doctors.

Megan was placed in the hospital in San Antonio, 220 miles from their home, on July 28th for constant bed rest and monitoring. We received the call on July 30th that one of the babies was in distress so they were going to take them that day, in the 26th week of pregnancy. This was about 14 weeks early.

Fast forward to Christmas – Madison and Mackenzie have been home for over two months and doing absolutely great – and (aside from sleep deprivation) Mom and Dad are doing great also.

That was a long and stressful three months for Cade and Megan; but the two young parents have plenty reasons to be proud of themselves. Megan was there, in the hospital, every day and Cade was there every time he could get away from work.

Many times, the great team of doctors and nurses performed some miraculous healthcare. These two "miracle babies" responded to every treatment like the real little "troupers" they are.

A lot of prayers were said every day by many folks, who will never know how much our family appreciates them. Throughout this very stressful time in our lives, there were also a lot of smiles and laughs.

For example, we laughed when Mackenzie managed to re-move her own ventilator on the second day – a sign of her "independent" personality. Only time will tell, but we think we might have been right on that one.

We also found humor when Madison progressed at a very steady pace without many issues, and took this as a sign of her "compliant and serious" personality. Again, only time will tell.

Prayers and the grace of God were really what got us all through this time. But humor and laughter was the gift God gave us to deal with it all daily.

Then I was diagnosed with Prostate Cancer and had surgery in August. Following surgery, a pathology report showed something called "positive margin," which meant maybe the surgery didn't get it all. As a precaution, I have been taking radiation treatments for about 6 weeks.

I happened to be in a Wal-mart when I received the call from the doctor about my biopsy being positive. I don't know why, but getting the big news in Wal-mart struck me as ironic. I had just commented to someone on Wal-mart's becoming a complete "one stop shop" with a McDonald's, a bank, hair salon, nail salon, pharmacy, picture studio, automotive repair, florist and garden, groceries, electronics, housewares, clothes, tools, baby items, crafts, bakery, and take-out. I'd heard some Wal-marts were even putting in dental offices and walk-in health clinics. I remember thinking how funny it would be to hear over the loud speaker, "Mr. Solsbery, please report to the Wal-mart Operating Room 3. Your prostate exam was positive!"

So you see, my sense of humor was up and running just about that fast. That's what happens when we program our Humor Attitude to always be on stand-by. Was it a serious time for me? Absolutely! But at the moment, it was all beyond my control so my job number one was to stay positive. And humor is one of the most positive frames of mind we can have.

My prognosis is very good, thank God. I consider radiation treatments as positive, and take them in stride, even finding little ways to inject humor into the situation. Just this week, I walked down the hall in my breezy little hospital gown wearing a red clown nose. Everyone was smiling and feeling better, at least for a moment.

Another update is the tough economic times. After opening the quarterly statement about my 401K a few days ago, I crossed out "401K" and replaced it with "201K" in big red letters. But happily I can see this big loss of money in the proper perspective: my net worth had taken a hit, but there will come a day when the situation will turn around.

I heard T. Boone Pickens being interviewed the other day about his reduction in net worth – a tad bit more than mine, I'm sure. Asked what he was doing differently during these tough economic times he said, "A year ago, the first thing I would do each day was to read the financial news and stock market report. Today, the first thing I did was read the 'funnies.' During times like these, we have to keep our sense of humor." Well said, Boone.

To me, a big part of the Humor Attitude is gratitude. And that's comes easily, because I'm such a fortunate man. Not only do I have a wonderful wife, a great son and daughter-in-law, two precious granddaughters, many friends, and a funny, neurotic dog; but I am indeed living my dream of being a professional speaker, who can help folks find the humor in their lives.

I've received a lot of encouragement and support along the way, and I thank God for all the people who are so generous with it. I also thank God for the gift of humor he gave us. I know, beyond the shadow of a doubt, that had I not made a conscious decision to use humor whenever it's appropriate, I wouldn't be enjoying this gift of life to its fullest!

Hope you have enjoyed reading this book as much as I've enjoyed writing it; that you had a few laughs and feel encouraged to apply The Humor Attitude to all things in your life. I can attest to the fact that the benefits are real!

To officially end this book, here's my final quote...

"Humor is an Attitude! Change the things you can, and laugh about the things you can't!"
Jim Bob Solsbery

Jim Bob's "Cutting Edge" Book Review Exercise

I'm sure you'd like to go through my book again, so I'll make it easier for you. Here are some questions you should be able to answer if you've been paying attention. It will remind you of the reading comprehension tests you took in school. But with my questions 1) there may be more than one correct answer, and 2) some of them have spaces for you to add your original answer. Good luck!

What companies or organizations use The Humor Attitude to improve their service?

a) Southwest Airlines
b) AT&T
c) The U.S. Government
d) Citi Bank
e) _____

Which American President was noted for having a great sense of humor?

a) William Howard Taft
b) Abraham Lincoln
c) Ronald Reagan
d) Jimmy Carter
e) Dwight Eisenhower

The problem with most self-help books is that:

a) they tend to focus on what is wrong with us
b) they're too expensive
c) they tend to sound the same
d) they spend little time focusing on what is "right" with us
e) _____

Male barn swallows prefer to have

a) darker colored breast feathers
b) larger nests
c) as few kids as possible

d) sesame seeds for breakfast
e) none of the above

How much of communication is non-verbal, according to experts?

a) 90 percent
b) 60 percent
c) About half
d) 25 percent
e) No comment

What happens if you burn more calories than you take in?

a) You begin to feel faint
b) You stop eating salads
c) You lose weight
d) Your social life begins to suffer
e) _____

What are some "terms of endearment" you can call those favorite dishes?

a) Thunder Thighs
b) Fat Fusion
c) Butt Builder
d) Chunky Cheeks
e) All of the above

How would you describe this book?

a) A self-help book
b) A humor book
c) A life balance book
d) A technical manual
e) _____

What were the "life lessons" in the "Manana" Robertson story?

a) A little rain makes it easier to plow
b) It gets harder to do things if we put them off
c) We should learn how to say "Whoa!"
d) We need to know when to say "Whoa!"
e) All of the above

When we talk to ourselves, what question should we ask ourselves?

a) "Does this mean I'm losing it?"
b) "Where did I leave my keys?"
c) "What's that guy's name again?"
d) "Does this mean I'm losing it?"
e) What exactly am I telling myself?"

After reading this book, we should start thinking of our lives as:

a) a series of funny stories
b) a big checkbook
c) a chance to make the world a little better
d) just one thing after another
e) _____

What's a good way to increase the fun at a family Christmas party?

a) Play charades
b) Look through old photo albums
c) Organize a caption contest
d) Prepare an extra dessert
e) _____

What is a strong family built around?

a) Love and acceptance
b) Making quality time
c) Finding ways to share a laugh
d) An ample supply of lawn chairs
e) _____

How much credit does Jan deserve for the success of her marriage?

a) 50%
b) 100%
c) 75%
d) 25%
e) However much she wants

What's a good reason to use a "humor trigger"?

a) To add humor to a conversation that's getting too tense
b) To reduce tension

c) To help untangle a tangled and clumsy subject
d) To help everybody put things in better perspective
e) _____

What's a great place to practice Self Deprecating humor?

a) The bedroom
b) The office
c) When speaking in public
d) In a courtroom
e) When you're asking someone for a favor

Which authors are most quoted in the book?

a) Winston Churchill
b) Lord Byron
c) Maya Angelou
d) Erma Bombeck
e) Will Rogers

What is mentioned in the book as a favorite comfort food?

a) Ice cream
b) Chocolate chip cookies
c) Mashed potatoes
d) Broccoli
e) Fried chicken

Who were Cuppy Graham's favorite singers?

a) Mel Torme and Tony Bennett
b) Dionne Warwick and Tina Turner
c) George Jones and Ray Price
d) Paul McCartney and Wings
e) Curt Cobain and Johnny Rotten

What made my father a good rancher?

a) His ability to choose good livestock
b) His good-looking children
c) His knowledge of the weather
d) Going broke before other ranchers
e) His ability to accept the things he could not control

ABOUT
JIM BOB SOLSBERY

Jim Bob Solsbery has over 25 years' experience as a successful business owner, entrepreneur, educator, national trainer, and Executive Director for the U. S. Department of Agriculture. This experience has given him the tools and resources to deliver programs that powerfully impact every audience.

Through Jim Bob's vast and varied experiences, he has discovered that successful, happy people share two traits – a positive attitude, and a healthy sense of humor.

The positive attitude leads to personal happiness, joy, and creative problem solving. Positive people are generous with praise, extend a smile, and are always on the lookout for the positive in any situation.

People who share a healthy sense of humor are happier, more productive, and better able to channel their positive energy into creative problem solving. A good sense of humor helps them resolve issues, improve relationships, and have a more positive outlook on life. For many of us, maintaining a healthy sense of humor and positive attitude requires some tweaking as we continue to fine tune our own behaviors. Many times we need to adjust our perspective and simply lighten up.

Jim Bob believes we sometimes make life too complicated. The successful role models in his life have proven to him that one can take their mission in life very seriously, yet take themselves lightly. He also believes humor, in the context of attitude, is a proven tool that directly relates to personal and professional success.

Jim Bob's presentations demonstrate his belief that humor is an integral part of life. He calls on his own personal experiences in Maryneal, Texas, to bring his messages to life, which makes his programs unique, entertaining, and informative.

Jim Bob's down-home humor and upbeat style will instantly connect with any crowd as he teaches audience members how to "laugh their way out!"

Jim Bob is a graduate of Texas A & M University, a Vietnam Veteran, and former educator and coach. He is retired from the U. S. Department of Agriculture where he served as an Executive Director and was also a National Trainer for new Executive Directors.

Jim Bob has presented to over 500 audiences and has received rave reviews. He likes to say, "I have never met an audience I didn't like!"

WANT TO BE A CONTRIBUTOR TO ONE OF JIM BOB'S UPCOMING BOOK PROJECTS?

Jim Bob is looking for contributors for a couple of upcoming book projects. Check out the projects below and decide what you may have to offer:

Humor Cookbook – Jim Bob is looking for recipes "with a sense of humor!" Send in any recipes of yours that have a funny name, a funny thing happened when you were cooking them, or a funny thing happened when you served them.

If they involve a funny story, send the story along with the recipes. Don't be shy! If there was ever a place that needs a laugh at times, it's the kitchen.

Real-life Humor Book – Jim Bob is compiling stories from audience members and readers of the times when something really funny happened to them or because of them, especially about times when humor "helped" the situation at hand or "helped" ease the tension.

The stories need to be true and original – after all, you will be given credit for the story. Let your memory go to work and get those stories submitted.

For either book, you will be contacted before your story or recipe is used; so make sure all your contact information is included – especially your email address.

Contributions should be submitted to:
Jim Bob Solsbery
jimbobspeaker@gmail.com
16706 Blue Shine Trail
Cypress, TX 77433

A message from Jim Bob to his Educator friends

Isn't it great to be in a profession that changes lives and builds brighter futures, every day?

As a superior educator, you're constantly growing. You're also rekindling the fire that keeps you in front of all those expectant kids, day in and day out. You need creative solutions to accomplish daily goals, a consistent way to apply those solutions, and motivation to apply them even on the days that seem to get away from you before you know it.

Jim Bob and Jan Solsbery are the team you need to make all that happen, and more. They have decades of experience "in the trenches," enriched by the latest information on how top educators stay ahead in your very challenging profession.

Jim Bob has been presenting educational keynotes and training sessions for over 10 years. He has spoken to over 40,000 educators. His wife, Jan, has 31 years' experience as a teacher and will be retiring soon. She has taught at every grade level from K through 12.

To learn more about their Education Programs and Training, please log on to www.TheEducationSpeaker.com. They would love to hear from you!

WHAT JIM BOB CAN DO FOR YOUR GROUP OR ORGANIZATION!

Humor is real important these days; we usually only get a few seconds to get people to give us a listen. Whatever you want to say, you'll make the most of those few seconds with a healthy dose of your Humor Attitude...and remember, few gifts are valued more than a happy smile!

Do you need to discuss something important with a co-worker, customer, boss or even a family member? Make it a pleasant discussion by showing off your Humor Attitude. Remember what Mary Poppins once sang, "A spoonful of sugar helps the medicine go down." Use humor only when appropriate, but use it every chance you get. You'll love the results!

Stress and worry can slow anybody down; but with the help of your Humor Attitude, you'll always stay on track and be optimistic. As funny lady Carol Burnett said, "Comedy is tragedy plus time." You can speed up anybody's recovery time by sharing your Humor Attitude – hey, you can even use it on yourself!

A Humor Attitude isn't something you do. It's about who you are. Get your Humor Attitude humming today; just tap into the wisdom and personal stories of a leading expert on the subject, Jim Bob Solsbery. You and your group or organization owe it to yourselves to start practicing Jim Bob's common sense techniques. In no time you'll be more productive, successful, appreciated...and happy.

Log on to www.LaughYourWayOut.com to find out more about how Jim Bob's presentations can benefit practically any group or organization. The Humor Attitude is universal, so it relates to audience members of all backgrounds.

THE AUTHOR WELCOMES
CORRESPONDENCE FROM READERS!

If you're looking for a speaker to energize and motivate your group, organization, business or school, Jim Bob Solsbery will get the job done.

For over 25 years, Jim Bob has been entertaining and motivating audiences with his down-home humor and upbeat style, which help him instantly connect with any crowd. Jim Bob is a home-spun philosopher of success, and his folksy wit takes us from his rural upbringing in Maryneal, Texas to today's fast-paced work environment. He shares principles and hysterical stories that center on his simple belief that we make life too complicated and that humor is more than laughter – it is an attitude!

Jim Bob's presentations are appropriate for a variety of audiences, including educators, associations, and businesses. Jim Bob's "listener-friendly" humor and stories relate to audience members of all backgrounds.

To inquire about booking Jim Bob to speak at your next event, please contact him at:

281-304-0861
jimbobspeaker@gmail.com
www.LaughYourWayOut.com
www.TheEducationSpeaker.com

Jim Bob also loves hearing from readers and audience members. If you have any inquiries, comments or compliments, feel free to write or email. Jim Bob will personally respond whenever he gets a break in his busy schedule. Jim Bob would also like to invite you to log on to his website and sign up for his FREE newsletter.

Order Form

Would you like more copies of *Humor Is An Attitude* to share with friends and family...or at least have a copy in each bathroom?

They can be ordered at www.LaughYourWayOut.com, or by mailing or faxing the order form below:

_____ YES. I would like to order _____ copies of *Humor Is An Attitude*.

_____ YES. I would like more information on Jim Bob's speaking fees and availability.

> Please send this form plus $15.00 for each book to the address or fax number below. Include $3.00 S&H for one book and $2.00 for each additional book.

My check or money order for $ _____ is enclosed.

Please charge my ❏ Visa ❏ MasterCard ❏ American Express

Name _____

Organization _____

Address _____

City/State/Zip _____

Phone _____ Email _____

Card # _____

Expiration Date _____ Signature _____

Call 281-304-0861
Fax Number 281-304-0871

Make checks payable and remit to:
Jim Bob Solsbery
16706 Blue Shine Trail
Cypress, TX 77433